TEACHING WRITING THROUGH THE IMMIGRANT STORY

TEACHING WRITING THROUGH THE IMMIGRANT STORY

EDITED BY
HEATHER OSTMAN,
HOWARD TINBERG,
AND DANIZETE MARTÍNEZ

UTAH STATE UNIVERSITY PRESS
Logan

Published by Utah State University Press
An imprint of University Press of Colorado
245 Century Circle, Suite 202
Louisville, Colorado 80027

 ASSOCIATION of UNIVERSITY PRESSES   The University Press of Colorado is a proud member of
the Association of University Presses.

The University Press of Colorado is a cooperative publishing enterprise supported,
in part, by Adams State University, Colorado State University, Fort Lewis College,
Metropolitan State University of Denver, University of Alaska Fairbanks, University
of Colorado, University of Denver, University of Northern Colorado, University of
Wyoming, Utah State University, and Western Colorado University.

∞ This paper meets the requirements of the ANSI/NISO Z39.48–1992
(Permanence of Paper)

ISBN: 978-1-64642-165-7 (paperback)
ISBN: 978-1-64642-166-4 (ebook)
https://doi.org/10.7330/9781646421664

Library of Congress Cataloging-in-Publication Data

Names: Ostman, Heather, editor. | Tinberg, Howard B., 1953– editor. |
    Martínez, Danizete, editor.
Title: Teaching writing through the immigrant story / edited by Heather Ostman,
    Howard Tinberg, and Danizete Martínez.
Description: Logan : Utah State University Press, [2021] | Includes bibliographical refer-
    ences and index.
Identifiers: LCCN 2021035729 (print) | LCCN 2021035730 (ebook) | ISBN
    9781646421657 (paperback ; alk. paper) | ISBN 9781646421664 (ebook)
Subjects: LCSH: English language—Rhetoric—Study and teaching (Higher)—Social
    aspects—United States. | Emigration and immigration—Study and teaching (Higher)—
    United States. | Social justice and education—United States. | LCGFT: Essays.
Classification: LCC PE1405.U6 T44 2021 (print) | LCC PE1405.U6 (ebook) |
    DDC 808/.042071173—dc23
LC record available at https://lccn.loc.gov/2021035729
LC ebook record available at https://lccn.loc.gov/2021035730

Cover illustration © Adelina ART

The editors dedicate *Teaching Writing through the Immigrant Story* to their parents:

To my parents, Grace Wood and Randolph Ostman, whose family stories span multiple nations but always lead to the same place, where love knows no boundaries.
—HEATHER OSTMAN

To my parents, who came to this country from the ashes of Europe to start life anew, following the Biblical commandment, "Go forth from your land and from your birthplace and from your father's house, to the land that I will show you."
—HOWARD TINBERG

To my mom, María Leude Patricio Ortega-Olson, who immigrated to the US from Brazil on wit, determination, and sass: "Para bom entendedor, meia palavra basta."
—DANIZETE MARTÍNEZ

CONTENTS

ACKNOWLEDGMENTS

The editors met while serving on the MLA Committee for Community Colleges several years ago. Under the leadership and direction of David Laurence, the committee was able to sponsor and support several conference panels dedicated to the literacy work that takes place in the nation's community colleges. We would like to thank David for his generosity, intelligence, and good nature, as he brought us together year after year to talk about our students and our institutions. We left each annual meeting rejuvenated and ready to continue the work of teaching writing in our respective colleges.

Additionally, we are grateful for the opportunity to be teachers at this moment in history, to be able to receive the gift of our students' learning. We extend our heartfelt thanks to each and every student we have had the privilege of teaching over the years; they are as much our teachers as we are theirs.

TEACHING WRITING THROUGH THE IMMIGRANT STORY

INTRODUCTION

Heather Ostman, Howard Tinberg, and Danizete Martínez

This project seems right for this moment. During an era marked by immigration conversations and arguments dominating nearly every public forum, the college classroom is, of course, not exempt. As our students struggle to make sense of a nation that alternates between hospitality and hostility toward multitudes of immigrants to its shores, we—their teachers—often find ourselves trying to navigate the same uneven waters at the very same time. As a result, as teachers we are learning with them and from them because, frankly, the topic of immigration is as political as it is personal. So many of us understand our lives and our families—our past, present, and future—within the contexts of our own immigrant journeys. Composition classes have always been a site for meaning making and deciphering meaning, as students work their ideas and knowledge into academic discourse, in addition to discovering themselves as thinkers and writers. Central to that discovery is the breadth of knowledge all students bring to the classroom, drawn from their previous educational experiences certainly, but, equally important, drawn from their life experiences prior to entering the composition classroom, which for nearly every student is shaped by a personal narrative about how they have come to *be* in that classroom. Certainly immigration, as a broad topic, offers students a way into understanding the world around them and a way for articulating their ideas and place within that world insofar as it is a common topic for discussion. Beyond its general accessibility, the lens of immigration also provides a viable frame for situating and articulating knowledge as well as building knowledge within and outside of the classroom.

But even beyond all of that, the topic of immigration as a pedagogical site of inquiry is not just current, it is urgent. Daily national and global forums engage the question of immigrants' rights and legitimacy—a nativist question that has emerged in waves over the centuries and one that is never quite put to rest as the United States attempts to make sense of its national identity amid a shift in global demographics. How any nation treats its new arrivals reflects everything about its regard for

https://doi.org/10.7330/9781646421664.c000

humanity: its public policies, its level of tolerance, its expectations of assimilation, its generosity, and at the very least, its level of fear of a perceived Other. As a topic that opens the discussion of the legitimization as well as the marginalization of the "Other," we have found that the immigrant story enables the opportunity to explore and evaluate the othering of learning spaces, particularly of nonacademic ways of knowing.

The chapters in this volume speak to the immigrant story as a viable frame for teaching writing—an opportunity for building and articulating knowledge through academic discourse—but the chapter authors access this occasion through the very real, very vivid, lives lived within and outside of the classroom. Each of the chapters in *Teaching Writing through the Immigrant Story* recognizes the prevalence of immigrant students present in writing classrooms across the United States (and we include foreign-born, first- and second-generation Americans, and more in this definition of immigrant) and the myriad opportunities and challenges those students present to their instructors, but each contributor here has also seen the absolute validity in the stories and experiences the students bring to the classroom—evidence of their lifetimes of complex learning in both academic and nonacademic settings. Further, the contributors themselves—like thousands of college-level instructors in the United States—have immigrant stories of their own. Therefore, the immigrant narrative—in its multiplicity of forms—offers a unique framework for knowledge production in which students and teachers may learn from each other, in which the ordinary power dynamic of teacher to students begins to shift, to allow empathy to emerge, and to provide space for an authentic kind of pedagogy, which, as Tara Fenwick has said, "like learning, is about struggle and invention, not certainty and control" (16). In these chapters, readers will find instructors who are willing to learn with their students, who demonstrate an openness to not knowing all of the answers but a solid commitment to creating a safe, constructive space to find them together.

The contributors to this volume, *Teaching Writing through the Immigrant Story*, offer a collection of essays that explores the intersection between immigration and pedagogy via the narrative form. Our collective work emerges within the contexts of student work, drawn from writing about or responding to immigrant stories, as well as from our own perspectives as immigrant, or as first- and second-generation immigrant, teachers. For each of the editors in particular, the topic of immigration is packed with significance on multiple levels beyond our professional concerns. For all of us, the topic is personal, as well as pedagogical, political, and urgent. For Heather, a first-generation American, family traditions shaped the road to college and beyond, but it was her work at the State University of New York, Westchester Community College, that codified her interest. In the college's surrounding community, where one in four county residents is foreign-born, she took for granted the multiplicities of identity and culture that appeared in her classrooms, and after teaching in a Eurocentric curriculum for years, she came to see the necessity of broadening the curricular approach to teaching by intentionally and explicitly including the immigrant experience. The immigrant experience offers a framework for the consideration of myriad knowledges and literacies that students present in the writing classroom, particularly as it serves as a reminder of all that is at stake in the classroom: the urgent social, cultural, economic, and political ramifications that stem from the ability to articulate knowledge into academic discourse.

For Howard, the immigrant's story and the call for social justice have deep resonance. A child of Holocaust survivors who were allowed into this country as refugees only after having lost virtually all of their family members during the war and having spent considerable time in a Displaced Persons camp in Germany, Howard has always felt an affinity for those seeking aid and comfort from beyond US borders. Moreover, having been reared in a traditional Jewish household in which the Bible held considerable sway, Howard had heard often (during services and during Passover seders) these deeply felt teachings: "Also thou shalt not oppress a stranger: for ye know the heart of a stranger, seeing ye were strangers in the land of Egypt" (*King James Bible*, Exodus 23.9) and "But the stranger that dwelleth with you shall be unto you as one born among you, and thou shalt love him as thyself, for ye were strangers in the land of Egypt" (Leviticus 19.34). Perhaps not surprisingly, Howard has spent more than three decades teaching full time at a public, open-access community college where the doors remain open to all.

For Danizete, also a first-generation American whose mother came to the United States from Brazil as a Fulbright Scholar, education has been central to her ethos in terms of citizenship and responsibility to her community. Having grown up in a Latino household in New Mexico with parents involved in the Chicano Civil Rights Movement and being deeply invested in education, Danizete has also dedicated her career to teaching at two-year open access institutions with historically Hispanic populations while researching Xicanx cultural production and the positionality of marginalized identities within the dominant culture.

While the editors teach at community colleges, the other contributors to this volume teach in various kinds of institutions ranging from community colleges in urban, suburban, and rural areas to four-year colleges and institutions, both public and private. Yet all of them—all of us—are confronted by the current political context of our age. Therefore, we have elected to focus on composition and credit-bearing courses as a unified platform for the variety of institutions represented among the essays, because composition courses very often function as gateway courses to a college education. We are aware that developmental writing courses prevail particularly among community colleges and offer a rich space for considering the immigrant story as a site of inquiry; however, given the multiplicity of competing issues that present in such courses, we have elected to address the intersections between "immigration" as a lens and developmental writing pedagogy elsewhere. For now, as college-level composition instructors, we are compelled by the narrative opportunities that have emerged in this context; as citizens in a democratic republic, we are equally compelled to help students negotiate those narrative opportunities and their own, supporting their active participation in a world that directly affects them—whether they are aware of those effects or not. Mostly, we know they are well aware. Thousands of our students are foreign-born or are the children or grandchildren of immigrants, so the effects land quite directly and personally. They know firsthand the struggles of establishing themselves or their family in a new land, one that is alternately welcoming and unfriendly. But, collectively, they challenge us to continue to try new pedagogical strategies and to learn more along with them. They inspire us with their willingness and trust in our classrooms, even as many of us struggle to make sense of the political climate we find ourselves in. Regardless of how any of us enter the classroom, we recognize our common responsibility: to teach our students with the best resources and intelligence we can muster. We know that everything depends on how well we execute our charge, because for so many of our students, *everything* depends on how well they do in college.

Organized into two parts, *Teaching Writing through the Immigrant Story* presents the interdependent issues of identity and pedagogy within the framework of the immigrant story. *Part 1: Situating the Discussion* opens the collection with writing instructors telling their own immigrant stories as a way of scaffolding the conversation: The topic of immigration in the classroom is as personal as it is political, a rich resource for the teaching of writing and critical thinking. For many, immigrant stories are the narrative threads that link prior knowledge to the present classroom experience; therefore, the contributors to this first part—as well as throughout this project—are not shy and do not apologize for drawing on their own prior learning experiences from their own lives, which have helped them understand who they are today as learners and educators. Because, as we all know, our stories as teachers inform everything we do in the classroom; our family histories and our personal journeys shape us as teachers, enabling us to see and hear our students, empowering us to respond and create. We tell our own stories so that, as contributor Elizabeth Stone says, ideally our students, our colleagues, and our readers might "recognize that there is more that connects us than separates us," in spite of how different we all seem from one another.

In chapter 1, "I am an Immigrant: Cultural Multiplicities in US Educational Systems," Sybille Gruber, a writing instructor originally from Austria, situates the immigrant story in terms of her own journey navigating cultures and literacies from one nation to another, as she "became part of the immigrant narrative," teaching in her adopted land of the United States of America. In this essay, Gruber reflects on the writing classroom with a specific focus on contradictory cultural positions and the rhetorical significance of identity, particularly through the dual lenses of teacher and immigrant, as she reveals herself as an instructor who, because of her own life's trajectory, is sensitized to the nuances of the immigrant student experience and who uses the classroom as an active space to use the immigrant story to mitigate the challenges of teaching writing and acclimating to a new culture. Through "asymmetrical reciprocity," which creates a space for difference as well as safe inquiry and learning within the classroom, Gruber discusses how she leverages this space as a place for building knowledge and strengthening her students' engagement with academic discourse.

The second chapter in our collection situates the discussion of the immigrant narrative in terms of teaching from the perspective of the perceived "Other," as Elizabeth Stone reveals her own family immigration story and the ways it emerges in the classroom and enhances her teaching. In "My Italian Grandmother, the Enemy Alien: Bringing Her Story and Others into My Classroom in an age of Nativism," Stone traces the history of her family's immigration as it opens up the critical possibilities for exploring the discourses of power and privilege, as her students negotiate that power firsthand in the academy. Through the lens of her own immigrant story, Stone shows how she and her students examine rhetorical strategies that marginalize the immigrant narrative as well as engage rhetorical strategies that claim/reclaim its legitimacy.

The third and final chapter in the first part of the collection, "Immigrant Stories from the Deep South: Stories of Bias, Discrimination, and Hope," by Liliana W. Mina with her students, Brittany Armstrong, Venijah Bellamy, and Paul Frick, provides a bridge from the teacher-centered narratives in Part 1 to the student-centered pedagogies that follow in Part 2. Mina's essay draws out the paradigm shift that is at the heart of this volume and that is explored and broadened in the essays that follow. In this chapter, Mina draws from both her students' as well as her own immigrant story in the classroom, employing a multiplicity of voices as she moves from self-narrative to research-based student writing. She narrates her experiences as an Egyptian immigrant instructor teaching in Alabama, as she studies and draws examples from her students' research and linguistic explorations across national, geographical, and emotional borders. In this essay, Mina and her students are all too aware of the immigrant student experience in which "immigrants find themselves obliged to discard, rather than build on, their existing resources," but as she notes, the authors collectively attempt to reverse this trend, and these efforts lead Mina to draw conclusions about and identify directions for American educational policies.

The chapters that follow in the second part of the volume, "Teaching through the Stories," build upon the earlier chapters' focus on the personal stories of instructors and expand outward more intentionally toward pedagogical practice that enables students and faculty to learn from each other. The essays in "Part 2: Teaching through the Stories" continue to build upon the intersections between identity and pedagogy and draw from literary sources and student writing to facilitate further student writing and critical thinking. The contributors to this section at times articulate strong political opinions about US immigration policy, and we, the editors, stand behind their right to articulate those opinions, particularly as they are attempting to strengthen their own students' critical thinking and ability to draw their own conclusions about society and their relationships to it, independent of their teachers' own ideas.

Therefore, chapter 4, "Reorienting via Triad: From Animals, Rapists, and Gang Members to Living, Breathing, Human Beings," by Katie Daily, draws from Danticat's fictional work as well as current journalistic texts to engage questions and issues emergent from detention centers, detainee medical treatments, and human rights and the ways students might approach these topics through writing. Using Danticat's work, Daily demonstrates strategies for enabling students' close readings and creating bridges for articulating their conclusions about the treatment—both political and health-related—of immigrants to the United States.

Chapter 5, "Initiating a Globally Inclusive Undergraduate Curriculum through Luis Valdez's Chicano/a Protest Theater," by Danizete Martínez, explores immigration on macro- and micro-levels. At first outlining the focus in her First-Year Composition course, the author delineates the rhetorical strategies found within selected Chicana literature, which foreground social injustice and inequality. Using student examples, Martínez then narrows her focus on pedagogical approaches to teaching Chicana drama through writing and reflective practice as they point to Chicana drama's contribution to efforts toward rethinking the American undergraduate curriculum.

In chapter 6, Tuli Chatterji posits Arjun Appadurai's essay "Disjuncture and Difference" as the foundation for a postcolonial composition pedagogical framework to explore how multilocal experiences initiate immigrant students to construct critical, complex discourses of hybridity. In the seventh chapter, Libby Garland and Emily Schnee address the political implications and contexts for writing in "Classrooms Filled with Stories: Writing Immigrant Narratives in the Age of Trump." In this chapter, the authors confront the high stakes of immigrant stories within the academic realm and the particular reflective effects and political challenges for teachers engaged in enabling students to write their stories.

In chapter 8, John C. Havard, Silvia Giagnoni, Timothy J. Henderson, Brennan Herring, and Rachel Pate develop an honors-level writing-intensive course around the immigrant experience with an explicit emphasis on the human element through synthesizing myriad forms of the immigrant story through the news, interviews with live subjects, and reflective writing. Designed as a requirement for the Auburn University Honors program, the course objectives include research and writing to deepen students' understanding of global citizenship, respect for cultural diversity, and engagement of social responsibility.

Finally, chapter 9, "Reflective Practice, Immigrant Narratives, and the Humanities Institute," by Heather Ostman, takes a broader look at enriching a humanities curriculum through student writing and reflective practice that draws from immigrant stories and creates the scaffolding for further knowledge production. The chapter emphasizes multiple pedagogical principles inherent in prior learning assessment, such as the centrality of situated or subordinated knowledge to legitimizing the immigrant story as a site of knowledge production and a viable means for accessing academic discourse through reflective practice.

Collectively, the chapters of *Teaching Writing through the Immigrant Story* extend and deepen a conversation that has already begun among colleagues at universities and colleges, as well as national and regional conferences, and that engages multiple facets of the immigrant experience in the United States and beyond. The contributors to this volume address teaching writing through the frame of the immigrant story, both as teachers of immigrant and native-born students and at times as immigrants themselves. The volume is timely, as immigration policies are under scrutiny by the federal government and lawmakers across the nation. Every university and college in the United States has students who are or will be affected by current or pending immigration legislation, such as the many DACA (Deferred Action for Childhood Arrivals) students enrolled in these institutions, who seek citizenship but already claim the United States of America as their home. The time is now to engage the topic of immigration as a framework for writing and critical thinking, particularly as it enables the prior learning experiences of students—and their teachers—to become central to knowledge production in the classroom.

Perhaps equally important, the lens of immigrant stories within the classroom also facilitates a necessary shift from the conventional, traditional learning paradigm in the composition classroom. By foregrounding the immigrant story, elevating it as a tool for learning, writing instructors and students create classroom space for knowledge production and academic discourse while learning from each other. Moreover, through this collection, we invite composition colleagues to leave a space in the classroom for students to tell their stories—especially personal stories of immigration—and by so doing sending students the message that they are more than consumers of texts and may produce and compose powerful texts of their own.

Scholars in composition, rhetoric, and in allied fields such as gender and critical race studies have for decades propounded the view that positionality matters—in how we construct the world and how we are constructed by others. The stories captured in this collection are framed through the experience of the storyteller—whether the students or the faculty. That fact matters and gives power and meaning to those stories. Vantage point matters. "How you construe is how you construct," the composition scholar Ann E. Berthoff observed many years ago (10). That maxim is no less true today and furthermore has application beyond the teaching of writing, capable of informing instruction not only in the humanities but in the social and technical sciences.

WORKS CITED

Berthoff, Ann E. *The Making of Meaning.* Boynton/Cook, 1981.
Fenwick, Tara. "The Audacity of Hope: Towards Poorer Pedagogies." *Studies in the Education of Adults* vol. 38, no. 1 (2006): 9–24.
The Holy Bible: King James Version. New American Library, 1974.

PART 1

Situating the Discussion

1

I AM AN IMMIGRANT
Cultural Multiplicities in US Educational Systems

Sibylle Gruber

INTRODUCING AN IMMIGRANT NARRATIVE

I became an immigrant many years ago. "Come visit any time," my uncle from America said during his visit to Austria in the early 1980s. He had left Austria in the 1950s and, after a detour to Australia, had become an American immigrant to "make a better life for himself." As an impressionable sixteen-year-old who grew up in a small rural town in Austria and who had heard many stories of my uncle's success in America, I held on to his invitation and, at the age of nineteen, booked an open-ended flight to Chicago. My family protested loudly, but I wanted to find out about the magic of America, where my uncle—whom I had seen only twice in my life but who always sent a ten-dollar bill for Christmas—had made a successful life for himself. I found a job as an undeclared and undocumented nanny-housekeeper, taking care of two very headstrong kids, a very big dog, and an even bigger house. I lasted for six months with little to no income in what I now understand was a hostile work environment.

When I returned to the United States five years later, this time as a Fulbright student from the University of Vienna, my experiences were very different from my nanny-housekeeper experiences in terms of what life could be in the United States. I enjoyed it much more, even though my English comprehension was much less nuanced in my first few years than it is now. After completing a master's degree and a doctorate in writing studies, I established my career as a professor of rhetoric and writing, and, even though I am not a US citizen, my family and friends make America my home.

In this article, I focus on my experiences as an immigrant to the United States to show the complexity of being different, the importance of looking at multicultural identities, and the need to look at individual experiences and struggles to create an understanding of how internationals, immigrants, and refugees are influenced by and also influence

https://doi.org/10.7330/9781646421664.c001

national narratives about difference and diversity. Specifically, I show that my struggles and my interpretations of my social, cultural, and political positionalities as an immigrant influence my work as a teacher on a daily basis. I show that my experiences with learning English and acquiring academic literacies, and my difficulties with fitting into a US system created multiple, shifting, and sometimes contradictory cultural positions that many internationals, immigrants, and refugees need to negotiate in order to be successful in their new temporary or permanent home country. I then address immigrant students' complicated position in the current US system before providing strategies to encourage learning opportunities for all students, using my experiences emigrating to the United States and teaching in a US educational system. I conclude by pointing out that discussions on identity development are especially important in a time when non-US students' rights are quickly disappearing. I point out that we need to educate ourselves so that all teachers can participate in working with immigrant, international, and refugee students who have to negotiate changing cultural paradigms, shifting perspectives on immigration, and sometimes hostile attitudes toward aliens, albeit ones from planet Earth.

A RETROSPECTIVE: REVISING CULTURAL AND SOCIAL IDENTITIES

Culture is often used to show a shared set of values, ideas, and rules for its members. Cultural norms differentiate one group from another group. Geert Hofstede, focusing on organizational cultures, tells us that culture "is the collective programming of the mind that distinguishes the members of one group or category of people from others" (3). It can refer to a nation, ethnic group, religious group, organization, and occupational group. Culture, however, is never stationary and never exists in a vacuum, but instead functions within specific norms and evolves and changes when norms change. Because culture is a socially constructed reality, this reality changes when different cultures meet and interact. Mary Louise Pratt explains this concept of the "contact zone" in her work on transculturation where she points out that "a contact perspective emphasizes how subjects are constituted in and by their relations to each other. It treats the relations among colonizers and colonized, or travelers and 'travelees,' not in terms of separateness or apartheid, but in terms of copresence, interaction, interlocking understanding and practices" (*Imperial Eyes* 7).

Contact zones, however, are rarely entered without preconceived notions of privilege and power. As Pierre Bourdieu explained in his 1977 work on "cultural reproduction and social reproduction," we privilege those whose cultural capital, which "consists mainly of linguistic and cultural competence" (494), is shared by the dominant culture. The majority of immigrants, even those who come on a specialized work visa, are seldom seen to exhibit the dominant culture's linguistic and cultural competence in their new country or to contribute successfully to established social frameworks by the majority group. Continuous attempts to close down the borders, build a wall between the United States and Mexico, restrict immigration from largely Muslim countries, backtrack on in-state tuition eligibility for DACA students, and deport Mexican immigrants, attest to the belief that the cultural capital of immigrants is not valued or welcomed by the US government. Immigrants are described as "aliens," "foreigners," and "outsiders," and they are seen as "exotic," "different," and "strange." Derogatory terms for immigrants include "rapists" and "criminals," and executive orders such as the "Executive Order Protecting the Nation from Foreign Terrorist Entry into The United States" on January 27, 2017 contribute to further dehumanizing attitudes toward immigrants.

The uproar caused by the order, the resulting protests, and the restraining orders upheld by the United States Court of Appeals for the Ninth Circuit on February 9, 2017, and on May 15, 2017, provided a more hopeful picture on immigration—at least for a few weeks. No longer the "problem," posters at the protests that I joined proclaimed that "refugees are welcome here," "I love my Muslim neighbor," "We are all immigrants," and "We can't unify with hate." Our language at the 2017 protest marches reflected Gloria Anzaldúa's belief in multiple and overlapping identities, a concept that she emphasized in *Borderlands/La Frontera* (99). Before immigrant and international students come to the United States and become part of the immigrant narrative, many are unaware of Anzaldúa's discussion of multiple identities and multiple cultural frameworks. For example, in my home country, I identified most strongly as a daughter, sister, friend, and student. I grew up Catholic in a small rural Austrian town of nine hundred people who socialized right outside the church doors before and after church service. My friends and I went to a small elementary school of twenty students. We knew each other well and shared many experiences and beliefs. My world remained small, and we never had a reason to question our nationality, our beliefs, and our values.

Even though international and immigrant students have widely differing experiences in their home countries, many of us learn that our lives become more complicated when we leave our known environments, even if the move doesn't involve physical border crossing. When I moved 120 kilometers east to Vienna for my university studies, my small world expanded drastically. I learned about city people and how differently they communicated. I learned about people from the western part of Austria and how hard it was to understand their dialects. I learned about people from different countries, and how difficult it was for them to speak German, and for me to find a common language. I also learned about assumed cultural norms, and how strange our Catholic customs were to internationals from non-Catholic countries. I grew up with a statue of a saint on every bridge, and a painting of a saint on many houses, creating a norm that was not widely shared beyond Europe's Catholic borders. It was the first time that I became conscious of difference, but it was a consciousness rooted in the knowledge that I was a member of the majority group whose identity was rooted deeply in many of the Austrian cultures—cultures that were neither questioned nor clearly articulated.

Similar to mainstream students in the United States or in other countries, I was a mainstream student in my own country. Because I was a member of the majority group, it wasn't necessary to dig deep and learn about inclusion and exclusion. It became necessary when I didn't fit into a preexisting system, and when I became a first-time immigrant to the United States. During my (mis)adventures as a nanny-housekeeper in the United States, my English language skills—acquired from an Austrian teacher, very accented, and grammatically passable—were abysmally inadequate as a communication tool. My farm experiences and my first language weren't helpful, and even though I had much to say, I wasn't able to express myself to the many kind and not-so-kind people I encountered during my initial introduction to the United States. Much like the experiences of our international and immigrant students, my life experiences were substantially different from those around me; I couldn't communicate successfully; I had never seen a big city with skyscrapers; I was not a member of the English-speaking majority group, and my economic situation was dismal.

Immigration to the United States, and a willingness to leave behind the known and familiar, is often connected to economic conditions, starting a better life, and creating opportunities we could not have in our home countries. Many of us don't come with money; many of us don't come with perfect English knowledge. When the six-year-old girl who was one of my charges in my nanny-housekeeper job said confidently: "You are different. You talk funny," I learned quickly that being different wasn't a good thing. The nannies spoke English with an accent, and even though some of us might have spoken with a preferred accent—Western European in general and French and British in particular—none of us were part of the mainstream culture that surrounded us. My accent kept me company during those years, and it made me different from the family for whom I worked, and the friends that they invited to the house. To them, I was invisible, voiceless, and powerless.

Accent alone did not relegate me to the powerless group of immigrants who have few resources to improve their situation and who encounter many roadblocks when trying to fight for their rights. Because I was an underpaid and overworked live-in nanny-housekeeper, my economic and social status, in conjunction with my accent, left little room for acceptance into the dominant mainstream culture. Like many new immigrants, I didn't have the language and academic training to understand the complicated system that keeps us in positions of disempowerment. Many years later, I would read the first edition of Rosina Lippi-Green's book on language ideology and discrimination in the United States, which put into words what I had no words for during my nanny life. My accent was a constant part of my daily life. It contributed to how I understood my place as an outsider. As Lippi-Green points out, having an accent often tells the speaker that they are different from the mainstream group. In her words, "accent becomes a litmus test for exclusion, an excuse to turn away, to refuse to recognize the other" (64). This refusal to engage with an accented speaker is reinforced by a standard language ideology that only exists as part of "an abstracted, idealized, homogenous spoken language" maintained by the upper-middle class (64).

I could claim whiteness and European cultural roots, attributes which Lippi-Green argues should have provided me with Bourdieu's "cultural capital" in the United States since it is "only accent linked to skin that isn't white, or which signals a third-world homeland, that evokes . . . negative reactions" (Lippi-Green 238–239). However, my inferior social and economic status associated with my position as domestic help, combined with my accent, diminished my cultural and social identity to one of "otherness." I was neither accepted nor welcomed by the dominant US culture, working twelve-hour days in an upper-class family who took social differences very seriously. I identified as an outsider, as somebody who was different from the dominant group, and as somebody who was silenced because of my inability to speak English without an accent in a socially inferior category. My accented English was not a positive attribute, and my low social status as "the help" exposed many stereotypes and prejudices.

Even though I looked and most likely sounded "white enough" (Lippi-Green 229)—a prerequisite for Lippi-Green's argument that accents from most Western European countries are considered acceptable by the dominant group—being white and from a European country was not enough when the point of the accented contact is clearly one of economic inferiority in a classist system.

My struggles with adjusting to a new cultural paradigm, my struggles with participating in a preexisting social system, and my struggles with communicating successfully are struggles that immigrant and international students encounter on a daily basis. We make sense of these hardships because we learn about others who have been in situations where their identities were questioned, undermined, and often dismantled. I am reminded of James Paul Gee and Michael Handford's comments on how we can comprehend of who we are, and who those around us are. Gee and Handford tell us that "people do not make meaning just as individuals. They do so as parts of social groups which agree on, contest, or negotiate norms and values about how language ought to be used and what things ought to mean" (5). During my life as a nanny-housekeeper, my world was limited to the house where I worked and to the country club where the family went to socialize with their friends. There was little opportunity to talk to other nanny-housekeepers freely and without being observed by the families who employed us. This meant that I could only make meaning from a very limited perspective because I did not have access to social groups that could help me contextualize my experiences in the United States.

I was lucky that, unlike many involuntary immigrants, I could escape from being a second-class alien. I could escape from a situation that undermined my self-worth. I didn't need to remain in a situation where monolingual English speakers spoke very loudly to make themselves better understood to foreign-language speakers, and where my intelligence was downgraded and equated with my accented and "broken" English. I could return to Austria where nobody would laugh at my language skills, and where I could communicate and express myself without being afraid that I would be misunderstood or that I would be categorized as "different" or "funny." My experiences as a hopeful immigrant who lost much of her hope, pride, dignity, and self-respect took some time to work through. However, once my environment changed to one where I could regain my self-confidence, my distressing experiences became learning and language experiences that pushed me to study English language and literature at the University of Vienna. If, as teachers, we can create learning environments that promote positive student self-perception, we can encourage participation and success not only for traditional US students but also for students whose positions as voluntary or involuntary immigrants and minorities make it more difficult to succeed in educational settings.

My initial experiences in the United States brought to the forefront the importance of paying attention to cultural values and cultural differences and to how identities develop and shift with experiences, interactions, and languages. Learning that my values were not shared, and that my status could move from insider to outsider very quickly and with little warning, encouraged me to focus my studies—in Austria and in the United States—on listening to and learning from nontraditional students whose languages and literacy practices were not sanctioned by the academy, and who often struggled to make their voices heard in the academic classroom. My own English skills had improved vastly from my first attempt in the United States, but my speech was accented and my writing was far from what academics would consider error-free. It was easiest to form new friendships with other international students who came from widely different political, social, and cultural backgrounds but who could relate to each other because we all lived outside the accepted mainstream norms. And even though Gloria Anzaldúa's concept of the borderlands was focused on US-Mexican relations, her discussion of living in the borderlands resonated with many of the internationals (194).

Some of us encountered racist stereotypes, some encountered language discrimination, and others dealt with xenophobic comments. All of us discussed and reflected on how we were treated, why we didn't fit in, how our discouraging interactions influenced our identities, and how attitudes, mindsets, and behaviors shifted and adjusted because of the new lives and new experiences we encountered. We became adept in juggling multiple identities, learning early on that discussions of politics are not welcomed everywhere, and that non-Western religious practices are often frowned upon, feared, or dismissed. I also learned to put aside some grievances, including students snickering at my accent, teachers happily pointing out that I used a wrong preposition, and some of my US colleagues and friends asking whether I would go home after finishing my studies so that I wouldn't take a job from the American students who graduated with me. It took me many years to feel part of the overall social, cultural, and political fabric of the United States, and I still have moments when I know that I am a foreigner, tolerated but not always accepted. Now, as a faculty member in a rhetoric department, I remember what it is like to be a first-generation immigrant, and I use my struggles and stories to address the experiences, concerns, and struggles of international, nontraditional, and immigrant students who are not sure about their place as students (and humans) in a country that has become less accepting and more hostile toward people who do not fit the mainstream narrative of US national identity.

CURRENT PERSPECTIVES: IMMIGRANT STUDENTS AT THE CROSSROADS

On September 5, 2017, Donald Trump called an end to Deferred Action for Childhood Arrivals (DACA), with Jeff Sessions supporting the decision and arguing that DACA "denied jobs to hundreds of thousands of Americans by allowing those same illegal aliens to take those jobs." Chuck Schumer, on the other hand, told reporters that this "heartless action" would be opposed by Democrats who "will do everything we can to prevent President Trump's terribly wrong order from becoming reality" (Senate Democrats, September 5, 2017). With a federal court order putting a hold on Trump's plan in January 2018, the Supreme Court declining to take up an appeal in February, an omnibus spending packet passed by congress that does not include DACA, and another court order in April 2018, close to 700,000 Dreamers will not be deported (Schmidt). However, the status of immigrant students is tentative at best. Trump's call for a wall between the United States and Mexico, his initial ban of Muslims from entering the United States, his call for an end to sanctuary cities, and his strong stance on deporting undocumented workers has not gone unnoticed in academic settings. Additionally, Arizona DACA students' revocation of their residence status has created a new challenge for immigrant students. Earl Johnson, vice president of enrollment and student services at the University of Tulsa in Oklahoma, in an article on the dropping number of international student visas, pointed out that "the current administration's 'America First' mantra is causing [immigrant/international students] a great deal of anxiety and fear" (quoted in Kavilanz).

Such anxiety and fear do not only deter students who want to study in the United States from applying to US colleges and universities. Immigrant students who are already in the country but don't have a residence card/Green Card or don't have citizenship have to negotiate daily interactions with their classmates, friends, and teachers. As new arrivals or as undocumented residents, immigrant students not only face a new learning environment once they enter college, they also face long-standing stereotypes and fears of family members being deported. In his discussion of immigrant reception, Reitz, for example, points out that immigrants have to contend with "pre-existing ethnic and race relations, labor markets and related institutions, government policies and programs both for immigration and for broader institutional regulation, and the changing nature of international boundaries" (Reitz 1006). Reitz, to address the complex nature of race and ethnicity, argues that "pre-existing ethnic attitudes, as well as inter-group boundaries and hierarchies, provide the social framework within which integration processes occur" (1008). New immigrants are often unprepared to address their own ethnic and racial backgrounds, whereas immigrants who grew up in the United States might only be too aware of how all-encompassing racial and ethnic differences can be. They are also aware of the anti-immigration changes advocated by the current US leadership. Whether documented or undocumented, the resulting heightened levels of stress and anxiety negatively influence school performance.

To counteract the negative impact of social, political, and cultural bias, Nguyen and Kebede argue that "school needs to be a positive place where immigrant students—whether foreign- or US-born, documented or undocumented—feel a strong sense of belonging and encouragement to move forward in the future" (723). For teachers, then, this means engaging with immigrant students not only in terms of their educational needs. Teachers also need to work with immigrant students to provide venues for their social, political, cultural, and religious needs. As an immigrant teacher especially, I want to make sure that I am an advocate for all students, and that I am also an advocate for immigrant students' right to be in the country and their right to have positive and constructive experiences as students and as members of their newly adopted country. Currently, immigrant students' concerns are especially focused on the anti-immigrant political climate, which, on January 20, 2017, became a focus of Trump's inaugural speech. To chants of "USA, USA, USA," Donald Trump declared that "a new vision will govern our land, from this day forward, it's going to be only America first." Students are still concerned about their undocumented families' fate in the United States and their own DACA status, their ability to renew their student visas, and their reception in communities where wearing a hijab can lead to anti-immigrant slurs from strangers. My own anxieties about my immigrant status were more pronounced during my most recent immigration status renewal than they had been in the past, and even though chances to be renewed were good, the current climate creates fear when fear should have no place.

PROMOTING AGENCY: IMMIGRATION, CULTURAL DIVERSITY, AND TEACHING

Teachers with the best intentions are sometimes unsure about how best to work with immigrant and international students. The diverse cultural, ethnic, social, religious, and political backgrounds are not always easy to navigate, and focusing on teaching to an amorphous middle is often easier than trying to figure out how to address diversity, language issues, and multiculturalism in the classroom and beyond. To integrate new arrivals or those who have been in the United States as immigrants for many years, I discuss some strategies for teachers that have helped me as an immigrant, an international student, and later as an immigrant faculty in the Southwest when I needed to navigate the complexities of a new language, new cultural paradigms, new historical and social frameworks, a new religious paradigm, a new educational system, and a new political system.

ASSUMING TOO MUCH: LEARNING FROM AND THROUGH EACH OTHER

Many of us have been told "I know what you mean!" or "That's exactly my experience!" And we have probably used those phrases ourselves when we want to affirm the comments of our friends, partners, or colleagues. However, I learned quickly during my international student years, where I spent much time with fellow internationals and immigrants from many different countries and very little time with American students, that we cannot know what another person really means. With this, I don't mean to say that we cannot communicate successfully about different experiences based on skin color, different religious practices, cultural stereotypes, or historical tensions. What I do mean is that I learned not to impose my interpretations and perspectives—based on my own social, cultural, and political knowledge—on the experiences of my international student friends. Instead, I learned to listen, ask questions, bring in my experiences, and engage in active dialogue to show that I appreciated and respected my fellow internationals' diverse perspectives. I learned about different religions, social and political systems, and complex race relations, and with it I grew and matured as a human being. We took from the discussions what was important to us, and we contributed to the discussions what mattered to us, changing our own reality to include bits and pieces of the stories that we heard.

Later in my educational career, I learned that Iris Marion Young, in her work on asymmetrical reciprocity, made a similar argument when she pointed to the dangers of assuming that we can know what another person experiences. Instead, she tells us, we need to listen carefully to another person's stories so that we can engage in dialogue, and through that dialogue, we can learn "about the narrative histories and interests," allowing us to "construct an account of the web of social relations that surround us and within which we act" (58). This way, we can learn more "about the other person's perspective" (53) without imposing our own perspective on the interactions.

Young's exploration of asymmetrical reciprocity—a shift from our understanding of symmetrical reciprocity discussed by Seyla Benhabib in her work on *Situating the Self*—entails an understanding "of equal respect and acknowledgment of one another," This, Young points out, "entails an acknowledgment of an asymmetry between subjects. While there may be many similarities and points of contact between them, each position and perspective transcend the others, goes beyond their possibility to share or imagine" (50). Because each member of a communicative exchange "brings to the relationships a history and structured positioning that makes them different from one another, with their own shape, trajectory, and configuration of forces" (50), it is especially important to participate in dialogue with "a sense of wonder." In that way, differences are not boundaries that prohibit interactions; instead, differences are approached as an opportunity to learn from each other and to share experiences that allow for different perspectives.

What this means for my interactions with students in our classrooms is that even though it is tempting to compare my experiences of being an immigrant faculty member to the experiences of current immigrant students, we do have to keep in mind that our experiences are also very different from our immigrant students' experiences. Keeping Young's discussion of asymmetry and sense of wonder in mind is especially important because of the diverse historical, cultural, social, religious, and political experiences of our students. However, we can engage in dialogue that encourages the exchange of knowledge, and with it the creation of new knowledge, based on the idea of "enlarged thought." Faculty whom I found especially approachable were those who didn't make assumptions about me based on my accent (Arnold would have been proud of me), the way I dressed (my town of 900 people didn't carry designer jeans), and what I considered punishment (office hours were only for those who were close to failing a class). Instead, they showed curiosity by asking questions, compassion by listening to the difficulties I was experiencing, and patience by explaining cultural beliefs that did not fit into my worldview. Similarly, in my interactions with students, I focus on ways to listen carefully, asking questions that show my interest without judgment, and bringing in experiences and stories from my own years as an immigrant to show points of connection without assuming points of sameness.

TEACHING AND POLITICS: CLASSROOM SPACES AS BIASED SPACES

Only a few years ago, a faculty member at my university ardently defended the university, and his classroom, as a neutral space where everybody could experience the same learning environment, and where politics should not enter. Such a perspective, however, assumes that the university and the classroom exist in isolation, separate from the real and undeniable issues affecting students and teachers every day. It denies students and faculty an opportunity to address civic engagement and responsibility as part of a student's learning process. These are certainly not new discussions; instead, they remind us of Paulo Freire's important work on teaching and learning as an act of empowerment. As he points out, students don't want teachers to talk "about reality as if it were motionless, static, compartmentalized, and predictable," leading to information that is "detached from reality, disconnected from the totality that engendered them and could give them significance" (71). Such an approach to education, he points out, feeds into the "ideology of oppression," an ideology that requires students to be mere "receiving objects" of education, with the intent "of indoctrinating them to adapt to the world of oppression" (78).

Freire's call to action, which ensures that students would no longer remain ignorant of their own power to change the world, has received much deserved attention in the United States (see, for example, Adams and Bell, Arao and Clemens, Bell, Buzzelli and Johnston, Giroux, Giroux and McLaren, Freire and Macedo, Smith). Freire's discussion of problem-posing education, critical consciousness, and critical pedagogy is especially pertinent when working with diverse students, including immigrant students, who are not part of the majority system. Without an understanding of their background, teachers would remain ignorant of students' needs. If, however, teachers learn about their students, each one is "no longer merely the-one-who-teaches, but one who is . . . taught in dialogue with the students, who in turn while being taught also teach" (80). They become jointly responsible for seeing education as essential for contributing to positive change in an unjust system. To use Freire's words, "Education as the practice of freedom—as opposed to education as the practice of domination—denies that man is abstract, isolated, independent, and unattached to the world; it also denies that the world exists as a reality apart from people" (81).

Freire's argument for education as a social and political act encourages students to "develop their power to perceive critically the way they exist in the world *with which* and *in which* they find themselves; they come to see the world not as a static reality, but as a reality in process, in transformation" (83, emphasis in original). The reality we live in currently is changing more rapidly than ever. Changes in DACA regulations are tweeted almost daily; new rules for Muslim refugees are broadcast and retracted; and Dreamers are unsure about the possible changes in their current status and the status of family members. Students at my institution have seen parents deported and are now living with relatives or friends. Instead of ignoring the social, cultural and political structures that influence immigrant students, it is now especially important to pay attention to how we can encourage them to become engaged students and members of their communities. Teaching critical thinking skills through a problem-posing pedagogical model allows us to provide students with opportunities to learn about and to participate in social action projects that are pertinent to them and to the larger community.

Immigrant students, and all students, need spaces where they can explore whether individual worries and fears are part of a larger systemic problem. During my student years, the classes that allowed for discussions on how students' individual positionalities fit into the larger social and political system became a place for addressing questions and concerns I had. More important, they also became spaces where we could make sense of our experiences, where we could discuss issues of social justice, and where we learned how to become part of a community that actively engaged in social action projects. Because I am an immigrant teacher, then, my classrooms are never neutral. I tell students that learning is a social process that is inevitably also political, and that we can never be silent bystanders to current injustices without contributing to those injustices. Classrooms, in my teaching, are spaces that encourage learning in conjunction with the world and not apart from the world. With this, I follow Paulo Freire's argument that "reading the world always precedes reading the word, and reading the word implies continually reading the world," (23), creating opportunities for students to reflect, discuss, and contribute to changes in current perceptions of the world.

The classroom, then, has to become an active space for a diverse student body, where civil rights are emphasized, and where all students can and are encouraged to participate in the learning process. I borrow from social justice education—closely connected to problem-posing education and critical pedagogy—to emphasize, as explained by Lee Anne Bell, the need for students to "develop self-awareness, knowledge, and processes to examine issues of justice/injustice in their personal lives, communities, institutions, and broader society" (4). Such an approach acknowledges that social groups do not exist on an equal playing field but are divided by privilege and power, creating dominant and advantaged groups, and subordinate and disadvantaged groups (9). Immigrant students, because of systemic discriminatory practices, are often members of several subordinate groups including religious groups, ethnic groups, and racial groups. Because of threats of deportation, concerns of nonrenewal of student and/or work visas, and unfamiliarity with the political, social, and cultural system, "making waves" is not the first agenda item on immigrants' list of the many tasks they need to complete. Classrooms have to become spaces where immigrant and international students can discuss, learn about, and engage with students and faculty in a noncombative and nonthreatening environment.

I DON'T UNDERSTAND YOU: LANGUAGE BARRIERS AS A REALITY

After I had lived in the United States for thirty years, an adult male at our public library shouted at me to leave the country if I didn't want to speak English. I was using Skype to talk to my family in Austria, and I wasn't prepared for the comment, nor was I prepared to respond to it at the time. My mom wanted to know what had just happened, and all I knew to say was "Ah, some crazy guy!" I don't think the situation would have warranted an explanation of Susan Dicker's discussions of language and identity, and her argument that language is a "shaper of personal and cultural identity" (1). Nor would it have helped me to point out that "norms and values of a culture are expressed through language" (4), and that the norms and values I embraced when I spoke to my family included a different set of guidelines from those I embraced in my day-to-day life in the US town that I now call home. Dicker tells us that language "not only gives people a way of identifying with their cultures, but also constitutes a means by which they identify people and cultures different from their own" (5). Similar to skin color, dress, religious practices, or gender, language differences can relegate students and teachers to a disadvantaged minority, especially when the language or the accent signifies countries and regions that are culturally, socially, or economically deemed inferior.

My accented and sometimes grammatically mangled English was not an asset during my college years in the United States, even though my imitation of an American accent was a great asset during my English studies at the University of Vienna where native American-English speakers were few. I didn't hear my accent until I was enrolled in a language lab where the only acceptable accent was the standard American accent. Even though my teachers thought that Arnold Schwarzenegger's strong Austrian accent was perfect for the Terminator movies, they didn't find my Austrian accent similarly appealing. Time spent in the language lab, listening to my own voice, listening to a Standard American English voice, and trying to imitate the Standard American English voice resulted in an almost complete adoption of a standard American English accent. I don't know whether I am most upset with my ESL teacher for erasing a major identity marker, or whether I am most upset that the erasure of my accent was accomplished with my full cooperation at a time when I wanted to be part of a standardization that I now consider misguided at best and xenophobic and anti-immigrant at worst. At the time, however, I hadn't learned about the connections between language, culture, and identity explained by Dicker, and I wasn't aware of "linguistic colonization" addressed by Juan Guerra. As he points out, the United States still has not achieved "linguistic equity, inclusion, and justice" (26), which, in the past few years, has become an even more distant dream of educators across the country. Instead, continuous English-only movements reinforce a hegemonic and hierarchical system that limits who can succeed, who can stay, and who is accepted in the United States.

For many international and immigrant students who were not raised with English as their dominant language, linguistic barriers are often a main reason for doing poorly in class. These barriers have adverse effects on student participation in class, on student understanding of how they fit into the classroom and the university, and on how their status as an ELL student influences their understanding of who they are as individuals and as members of their communities. Fellow students with solid standard English language skills generally don't want to work with ELL students on their teams, and teachers are not interested in trying to understand accented English with innovative sentence constructions; they consider grading papers submitted by ELL students as a punishment. No longer is it a matter of checking whether a student understood the content, but it becomes a matter of whether a student can communicate and write in Standard American English.

Such difficulties are not only part of ELL students' experiences but are also common when working with disenfranchised US students who face similar difficulties when entering US college classrooms. Whether students' communication strategies are influenced by cultural and social differences or by language differences, disenfranchised students don't fit mainstream understandings of literacy practices. Common practices, as Juan Guerra points out, ask teachers to demystify academic language "to make it easier for students to adapt to an array of academic discourses that grant little opportunity for the integration of the linguistic practices or the lived experiences students bring with them" (36). During my ELL student career, standard American English language practices were the only ones accepted by my teachers, contributing to my unwillingness to speak up in class or to incorporate complex sentences to express some of the complex ideas I wanted to include in my essays.

As a teacher, I am very careful to consider the cultural and linguistic backgrounds of the students in my classroom. Not all of them are mainstream/standard American English speakers. Most of them, in fact, are learning to imitate discourse conventions required of them in different academic disciplines, starting with introductory composition courses and ending with their disciplinary capstone courses. How quickly students adapt to disciplinary requirements differs depending on how closely related their primary discourses—their home languages—are with their secondary discourses. In Gee's words, discourses are "ideological" and "are intimately related to the distribution of social power and hierarchical structure in society" (31), disadvantaging those who are outside the accepted standard used by the majority of participants in a given discourse community. For ELL and disenfranchised students, the adjustment is much more difficult if teachers do not recognize how students' home languages are linked to their understanding of themselves and of their performance in the classroom, and also to their acquisition of a new language or of new discourse conventions. However, according to Juan Guerra, we cannot simply encourage students to gain "critical awareness of how language works in varied contexts" (37) because such an approach perpetuates an idealized version of standard language performance. Instead, teachers need to pay attention that the values and viewpoints put forward by one discourse can, as James Gee points out, "marginalize viewpoints and values central to other discourses" (5).

For teachers, then, if we want to encourage all participants to continuously learn from each other, we also need to establish that language is constantly shifting based on discursive acts performed on an ongoing basis by widely diverse participants in specific communication endeavors. We also need to acknowledge that all students are welcomed members of the learning environment with contributions that enrich the learning experience. In my classroom, this starts with learning students' names in the respective languages with which they grew up. Ricardo does not become Richard, Eriberto is not renamed Herbert, and Yingyong does not become Lily. I use Spanish, English, French, and German phrases if appropriate, and students learn a few words in the languages represented in class. We talk about students' hometowns and home countries, not taking for granted that we know what it means to grow up in a small rural town in Arizona, a border town in Mexico, or a megalopolis in China. Language becomes part of a student's social and cultural identity, and new discourse strategies are learned as a way to consciously "navigate and negotiate the curricular and pedagogical spaces they inhabit in our college classrooms, across our campuses, and in an array of other communities of belonging" (Guerra 37). Students learn to use their linguistic resources in conjunction with their cultural resources, with much effort placed on acknowledging diverse language practices while also engaging in "rhetorically savvy" (41) practices that allow students to succeed in their respective college careers, their communities, and in their jobs.

COMMUNITY BUILDING: GLOBAL LEARNING AND BELONGING

For many years after I came to the United States, I most closely associated with non-US citizens. Most important in our search for a new community away from our home countries was the sense of belonging we found with each other. Our motley crew of internationals included Panamanians, Australians, Mexicans, South Africans, Italians, Brazilians, Swiss, Chinese, New Zealanders, Spaniards, Kenyans, Taiwanese, Indians, and a few Austrians. We identified as Internationals, and our group identity was understood as "different from" the group identity of US natives. We knew that, as a group of internationals, we couldn't be more different from each other, and that our commonalities were created because we all felt displaced. We didn't speak the same languages, we came from various cultural and social systems, and our political views were often incompatible. However, we all shared experiences based on being newcomers to a system that was foreign, sometimes hostile, and often incomprehensible. We needed to navigate a new educational system, and we depended on feedback and encouragement from others who had just learned the system and who could give us tips on how to participate in class, when to raise our hand, what to do when we are called into a teacher's office, and how to work with classmates. We didn't have social security cards or American driver's licenses, and we learned from each other how to talk to and not be intimidated by US officials. We also learned that American students were mostly very friendly but would hardly ever have time to go for the promised tea or coffee.

What I learned from our motley community was that each member of the group had much to contribute to the general knowledge of what it means to be part of a newcomer community. We understood that "difference" encompassed our countries of origin, our ethnicities, our economic statuses, our cultural backgrounds, and our languages. As members of the community of internationals, however, we learned from each other and we looked for commonalities instead of differences. We engaged, without knowing it, in what Shi-xu called "culturally diverse ways of knowledge-seeking," a practice that I now encourage in my role as a teacher. Shi-xu argues that a multicultural approach to systems of knowledge will help us grow as individuals because "we become more sensitive to the new complexities and dynamic changes taking place in globalized contemporary culture and discourse" (646). In other words, the importance of interacting with and learning from diverse individuals is especially important because globalization promotes interaction across different discourses and encourages new discourse conventions to take shape.

As a teacher, I encourage community building. I also encourage the coexistence of diverse discourses within communities, and the creation of new discourses by emphasizing and by celebrating the changing identity of the United States. Instead of subscribing to "standard" or "dominant" discourses, students focus on the effects of new traditions, cultural and religious practices, multilingualism, and the impact of globalization on communication practices. Because of renewed efforts to promote a singular national identity without considering the many diverse identities represented in the United States, it is especially important to incorporate international, nontraditional United States, and immigrant perspectives and experiences into the curriculum. Students in my classes are often asked to bring their own stories and backgrounds into the classroom to contextualize their experiences in the classroom and in the United States. They also conduct interviews that focus on immigrant stories and that complicate easy assumptions of who came to the United States, what the reasons were, and how they managed as new immigrants or as immigrants who have lived in the United States for many years. Students who see themselves as members of the classroom community learn from each other's stories, and also from those that they researched. This helps them create a framework that allows for multiple lenses when exploring difficult issues such as constantly changing immigration policies, refugee rights, and US customs and border control. Respect for and understanding of each other in a multicultural community, in other words, is no longer taught as a topic. Instead, it becomes a daily practice that connects all discussions in the classroom.

SAFE AND BRAVE SPACES: PROMOTING DIVERSITY AND RESISTING FEAR

My safe space was a multicultural space. It revolved around the international student community and not around classroom spaces. We learned from and with a diverse group of community members who were willing to share their sometimes conflicting experiences without making value judgments. We explored "contact zones," described by Pratt as "social spaces where cultures meet, clash, and grapple with each other" ("Arts of the" 32). Our contact zones were many and changed our understanding of each other and also of ourselves. We created places for "mutual recognition, safe houses in which to construct shared understandings, knowledges, claims on the world" (40). Rarely did our interactions become contentious, even though we understood major abstract concepts such as liberty, democracy, and morality very differently.

We also learned that meetings in contact zones are often "in contexts of highly asymmetrical relations of power" (32). One of these asymmetrical contact zones was inevitably the American classroom, especially where we couldn't hide in a big lecture hall but where we were expected to interact with teachers and classmates. Many of us came from systems where lectures were still the accepted norm, and where learning meant repeating lecture notes in exam situations. We were reluctant to engage in discussions where we could agree or disagree with the instructor, or where we could show that our thinking about a new concept was still in the beginning stages and needed to be fleshed out much more carefully. But nonparticipation was often associated with not being engaged, not having done the readings, or not being able to comprehend the readings. We did not feel safe, and we did not feel brave enough to explain to our teachers why we did not participate or engage in the discussions.

Because of my experiences as an international student, I now promote a wide variety of participatory opportunities. Instead of expecting every student to know what my expectations are about classroom interactions, I explain why it is important to participate in classroom activities, and what opportunities students have for interacting with me and with each other. Because international, immigrant, and nonmainstream students bring with them many different approaches to "correct" classroom behavior, it is especially important to create a space that is nonjudgmental and nonthreatening. Some students are comfortable raising their hand and answering questions on the spot, some need to think through their responses and write their answers first, some need to translate their answer from their home language before they feel comfortable participating, some need to talk in groups, and some prefer to take notes and use the discussion points in an online response. To create a successful and safe learning space, all of them need to feel a sense of belonging, where contributions are not seen as inferior or superior, and where learning and knowledge acquisition transform all students. This can lead to a diversity of perspectives that would otherwise not have been possible to achieve.

Classroom spaces, then, become contact zones that are also safe spaces, defined by Holley and Steiner as "an environment in which students are willing and able to participate and honestly struggle with challenging issues" (49). For teaching, this means that group membership is inclusive, and everybody contributes to knowledge making. Integration into the US educational system becomes a positive experience, without expecting that students automatically know what it means to be a student in the US educational system. It can also move students from safe spaces to what Boostrom calls "brave spaces"—spaces that encourage students to participate in new knowledge making and leaving old knowledge behind. As Boostrom argues, "learning necessarily involves not merely risk, but the pain of giving up a former condition in favour of a new way of seeing things" (399). Such an approach, as Arao and Clemens point out, allows for the disruption of dominant narratives where "knowledge flows one way from teachers to students" (142). Instead, all students—not only those who conform to dominant standards—contribute to, change, and increase our knowledge base in a safe and brave space with students as shapers and change agents of history.

WHAT WILL THE FUTURE HOLD: IMMIGRATION AND THE POWER OF MANY

Immigrants in the United States face complex and often demoralizing issues. The volatile political system, cultural differences, race relations, and increased xenophobia expressed by "America first" slogans create systems of stress and fear that influence the development, expression, cultivation, and transformation of immigrants' cultural, social, religious, or political identities. The June 22, 2020, presidential "Proclamation Suspending Entry of Aliens Who Present a Risk to the U.S. Labor Market Following the Coronavirus Outbreak" is one of the latest examples of new restrictions to immigrant workers. The rapid changes in social and political movements in the United States influence learning environments, social interactions, and cultural exchange in international and immigrant communities. They promote a continuation of systems that, as Lilia Monzó points out in an article on Latinx immigrant students, perpetuate a normative and hegemonic status where "the dominant group controls the production of accepted and commonsense knowledge and ideologies that become deeply embedded in our institutions and cultural practices" (149).

Immigrant faculty, with their own complex histories in their own countries and their adopted country, can and should promote students' right to an education that endorses and applies cultural heterogeneity as an embedded pedagogical tool. Such an approach can encourage all students to participate in developing social, cultural, and political frameworks that open doors for immigrants, internationals, and refugees. Immigrant faculty can and should become advocates for students from nonmainstream and non-US cultures and create spaces that encourage engagement with, learning from, and reenvisioning of the US educational system. This can then create opportunities for changing the current US national identity and challenging a cultural, social, economic, and political system where affluent Anglo US citizens benefit from societal advantages that are often unattainable for immigrants, ethnic minorities, and low-income US citizens.

Certainly, much work still needs to be done to ensure that all students can participate successfully in the learning process and in their future aspirations. Teacher training, administrator support, and community involvement are necessary to create living and learning environments that allow us to "open the door to the American dream." In a report on higher education access and success of immigrants conducted by the Institute for Higher Education Policy and Lumina Foundation for Education, Wendy Erisman and Shannon Looney argue that "developing a broader and more efficient path to citizenship and offering accessible and affordable programs to help immigrants learn English and become familiar with their new country would open the doors to higher education for many immigrants" (7). If we want to encourage opportunities for students to reimagine and rewrite a currently divisive US national narrative that encourages stereotyping, misinformation, and isolationism, then it is essential for immigrant faculty to bring into the classroom their own stories of coming to the United States, of being outside the mainstream, of struggling with a new language, or of creating safe spaces. And it is essential for all faculty to include learning practices that encourage discussions of the changing faces of the United States, engagement in diverse and changing communities, and participation in the many social and cultural events that define a multicultural and heterogeneous nation. As Caryn McTighe Musil tells us so forcefully, "If Lady Liberty is to avoid being on the run rather than under construction, students and others will need to study, refine values, and hone skills so they are prepared to act in collaboration to protect her" (Musil).

WORKS CITED

Adams, Maurianne, and Lee Anne Bell, editors. *Teaching for Diversity and Social Justice*, 3rd ed. Routledge, 2016.

Anzaldúa, Gloria. *Borderlands/La Frontera: The New Mestiza*. Aunt Lute Books, 1987.

Arao, Brian, and Kristi Clemens. "From Safe Spaces to Brave Spaces." *The Art of Effective Facilitation: Reflections from Social Justice Educators*, edited by Lisa M. Landreman, Stylus Publishing, 2013, pp. 135–150.

Bell, Lee Anne. "Theoretical Foundations for Social Justice Education." *Teaching for Diversity and Social Justice*, edited by Maurianne Adams and Lee Anne Bell, 3rd ed. Routledge, 2016, pp. 25–38.

Benhabib, Seyla. *Situating the Self: Gender, Community, and Postmodernism in Contemporary Ethics*. Psychology Press, 1992.

Boostrom, Robert. "The Student as Moral Agent." *Journal of Moral Education*, vol. 27, no. 2, 1998, pp. 179–190.

Bourdieu, Pierre. "Cultural Reproduction and Social Reproduction." *Power and Ideology in Education*, edited by Jerome Karabel and AH Halsey, Oxford University Press, 1977, pp. 487–511.

Buzzelli, Cary, and Bill Johnston. *The Moral Dimensions of Teaching: Language, Power, and Culture in Classroom Interaction*. Routledge, 2014.

Dicker, Susan J. *Languages in America: A Pluralist View*, 2nd ed. Multilingual Matters, 2003.

Erisman, Wendy, and Shannon Looney. "Opening the Door to the American Dream: Increasing Higher Education Access and Success for Immigrants." *Institute for Higher Education Policy and Lumina Foundation*, 2007, http://www.ihep.org/sites/default /files/uploads/docs/pubs/openingthedoor.pdf. Accessed 11 May 2021.

Freire, Paulo. *Pedagogy of the Oppressed. Continuum*, 1970.

Freire, Paulo, and Donaldo Macedo. *Literacy: Reading the Word and the World*. Bergin & Garvey, 1987.

Gee, James Paul. "What Is Literacy?" *Teaching and Learning*, vol. 2, 1987, pp. 3–11.

Gee, James Paul, and Michael Handford, editors. *The Routledge Handbook of Discourse Analysis*. Routledge, 2013.

Giroux, Henry A. *Border Crossings: Cultural Workers and the Politics of Education*, 2nd ed. Routledge, 2007.

Giroux, Henry A., and Peter McLaren, editors. *Between Borders: Pedagogy and the Politics of Cultural Studies*. Routledge, 1994.

Guerra, Juan C. *Language, Culture, Identity and Citizenship in College Classrooms and Communities*. Routledge, 2015.

Hofstede, Geert. "Dimensionalizing Cultures: The Hofstede Model in Context." *Online Readings in Psychology and Culture*, vol. 2, no. 1, 2011, pp. 3–26, https://scholarworks.gvsu.edu/cgi/viewcontent.cgi?article=1014&context=orpc. Accessed 11 May 2021.

Holley, Lynn C., and Sue Steiner. "Safe Space: Student Perspectives on Classroom Environment." *Journal of Social Work Education*, vol. 41, no. 1, 2005, pp. 49–64.

Kavilanz, Parija. "Sharp Drop in International Student Visas Worries Some US Colleges." *CNN Money*, 14 Mar. 2018, https://money.cnn.com/2018/03/12/news/economy/international-student-visa-college/index.html. Accessed 11 May 2021.

Lippi-Green, Rosina. *English with an Accent: Language, Ideology and Discrimination in the United States*, 2nd ed. Routledge, 2012.

Monzó, Lilia D. "'They Don't Know Anything!' Latinx Immigrant Students Appropriating the Oppressor's Voice." *Anthropology and Education Quarterly*, vol. 47, no. 2, 2016, pp. 148–166.

Musil, Caryn McTighe. "Clashes over Citizenship: Lady Liberty, Under Construction or On the Run?" *Diversity and Democracy*, vol. 20, no. 1, 2017, https://www.aacu.org/diversitydemocracy/2017/winter/musil. Accessed 11 May 2021.

Nguyen, Chi, and Maraki Kebede. "Immigrant Students in the Trump Era: What We Know and Do Not Know." *Educational Policy*, vol. 31, no. 6, 2017, pp. 716–742.

Pratt, Mary Louise. "Arts of the Contact Zone." *Profession*, 1991, pp. 33–40.

Pratt, Mary Louise. *Imperial Eyes: Travel Writing and Transculturation*. Routledge, 1992.

Reitz, Jeffrey G. "Host Societies and the Reception of Immigrants: Research Themes, Emerging Theories and Methodological Issues." *International Migration Review*, vol. 36, no. 4, 2002, pp. 1005–1019.

Schmidt, Samantha. "Trump Said 'DACA Is Dead,' but His Administration Has Approved 55,000 Applications Just This Year." *Washington Post*, 3 Apr. 2018. https://www.washingtonpost.com/news/morning-mix/wp/2018/04/03/trump-said-daca-is-dead-but-his-administration-approved-55000-applications-just-this-year/?noredirect=on&utm_term=.a472f7391276. Accessed 11 May 2021.

Senate Democrats. "Schumer Statement on Trump Administration Decision to End DACA." *Senate Democrats*, 5 Sep. 2017. https://www.democrats.senate.gov/newsroom/press-releases/schumer-statement-on-trump-administration-decision-to-end-daca. Accessed 11 May 2021.

Shi-xu. "A Multicultural Approach to Discourse Studies." *The Routledge Handbook of Discourse Analysis*, edited by James Paul Gee and Michael Handford, Routledge, 2013, pp. 642–653.

Smith, Andrea. "Native Studies and Critical Pedagogy: Beyond the Academic-Industrial Complex." *Activist Scholarship: Antiracism, Feminism, and Social Change*, edited by Julia Sudbury and Margo Okazawa-Rey, Paradigm Publishers, 2009, pp. 47–64.

Trump, Donald. "Proclamation Suspending Entry of Aliens Who Present a Risk to the U.S. Labor Market Following the Coronavirus Outbreak." Whitehouse Proclamation, 22 Jun. 2020, https://www.whitehouse.gov/presidential-actions/proclamation-suspending-entry-aliens-present-risk-u-s-labor-market-following-coronavirus-outbreak/. Accessed 2 July 2020.

United States, Executive Office of the President [Donald Trump]. Executive Order Protecting the Nation from Foreign Terrorist Entry into the United States. 27 Jan. 2017. *Trump White House Archives*, https://trumpwhitehouse.archives.gov/presidential-actions/executive-order-protecting-nation-foreign-terrorist-entry-united-states/. Accessed 2 July 2020.

United States, Court of Appeals for The Ninth Circuit. *Washington State v. Donald J. Trump*. 9 Feb. 2017. *United States Cours of Appeals for The Ninth Circuit*, https://cdn.ca9.uscourts.gov/datastore/opinions/2017/02/09/17-35105.pdf. Accessed 11 May 2021.

Young, Iris Marion. *Intersecting Voices: Dilemmas of Gender, Political Philosophy, and Policy*. Princeton University Press, 1997.

2

MY ITALIAN GRANDMOTHER, THE ENEMY ALIEN
Bringing Her Story and Others into My Classroom in an Age of Nativism

Elizabeth Stone

"I hope I didn't offend you," said one of my students, approaching my desk at the end of class one day, referring back to a question he'd asked earlier, "but I'd been wondering for a while about your interest in immigrants and immigration."

The class he was enrolled in, one of several that satisfy my college's pluralism requirement, is a literature course I designed on contemporary immigrant literature, and it includes fiction and/or nonfiction by Chimamanda Ngozi Adichie, Lan Samantha Chang, Edwidge Danticat, Junot Díaz, Cristina Garcia, Jhumpa Lahiri, Chang-Rae Lee, Bharati Mukherjee, as well as films, such as *Balseros*, a documentary about Cuban immigrants, and *The Visitor*, a feature film about the deportation of a Syrian without a valid visa.

Not surprisingly, the course appeals to many students from immigrant families. Whenever I offer the course, many of the students, including my interlocutor that day, are from families that have come to the United States post-1965, most being Afro-Caribbean, Asian, Latino, Middle Eastern, or South Asian, and most self-identifying as non-white. Before Donald Trump's candidacy and then presidency, the focus of the course had been on issues like transnationalism, or how immigration had placed challenges on parental authority and marital roles. Our texts also prompted discussions related to bilingualism and assimilation as revealed in the texts.

However, Trump's provocative nativist speeches spelling out his plans—to deport undocumented residents, especially Mexicans, Hondurans, Guatemalans, and Salvadorans; to bar Muslims from the country; to reconsider "birthright" citizenship; and to constrict the laws protecting asylees, refugees and those with temporary protective

https://doi.org/10.7330/9781646421664.c002

status (TPS)—often led us out of the texts, into the news, a deeper exploration of immigration law and sometimes back to their own personal experiences.

On this particular day, my student had wondered aloud why someone like me—a white woman with a European-sounding first and last name—would be drawn to literature written mainly by writers from non-white non-European immigrant families who arrived after 1965 and further, why, in an age of identity politics, I would be engaged by issues that didn't affect me personally. At a time when most students are familiar with concepts such as intersectionality, cultural appropriation, white fragility, and white privilege, I felt my student's question was legitimate and deserved an answer.

The following day, with my student's permission, I shared his question with the class, telling them that the answer was I came with an ethnic history of my own, invisible though it might be to them, that had long ago drawn me to the immigrant experience and that had eventually prompted me to design this English elective. I was the granddaughter of immigrants from the Aeolian Islands just north of Sicily in Southern Italy. My grandfather, Gaetano Bongiorno, first arrived in the United States in 1895. After ten years, he returned home to request permission to marry my grandmother, Annunziata, coming back with her in 1905. It was, I explained, a period of anti-immigrant nativism every bit as intense and vitriolic as the one we're living through now, when Italians and Eastern European Jews felt as unwelcome in the United States as Latinos and Muslims do today. (My father's parents were Eastern European Jews, and my father eventually changed his birth surname—Stein—to Stone, but that's a different story.)

I was a postwar baby boomer, and by the time I was born my Bongiorno grandfather had died, but my grandmother and her six children were storytellers, so I got to be part of a large extended family conversation about their lives in America that had begun with my grandparents' arrival. I was fascinated by the family stories they told and retold about their lives, stories often revolving around being Italians in anti-Italian America. In fact, my years sitting at my grandmother's dining room table was central to my interest not only in writing about the Italian-American experience (Stone, *Black Sheep*), but also in my scholarly work on family stories as a protective resource for families ("It's Still Hard").

I came of age in a period when the favored ideology was assimilation rather than the pluralism and transnationalism more familiar to my students. However, the rise of nativism actually made my own family background more pertinent to my students' experience than it had been. I realized I could use pertinent stories my family told as well as my contextualized knowledge of immigration politics and culture during the first quarter of the twentieth century—the formative period for my grandparents as immigrants and my mother's generation as children of immigrants—to bring that past to life and to show its parallels to the present. In that way, I could help my classes to see that the current nativist moment was not an anomaly. In fact, the strategies used today to stigmatize immigrants repeated rhetorical strategies dating at least as far back as the mid-eighteenth century.

Zeitgeists change, so no generation fully understands or can understand the experiences of previous generations. None of my students, for example, were familiar with the term WASP as an acronym for White Anglo-Saxon Protestant. For them, "whiteness" meant European, and it was monolithic. I therefore decided that for the duration of the course, in an *ad hoc* fashion, I would use myself as a resource, where pertinent, drawing on my family's stories dating back to the first part of the twentieth century as well as my research on immigration from that period. Because I was able to recount stories actually told to me long ago by relatives—which in the present moment meant events that had occurred more than a century ago!—it sometimes felt, even to me, as if I were bringing reports from a séance.

I knew from both experience and research that families under siege use their family stories privately and protectively. I also knew that in these stories, which may travel down the generations, (in Native American and African American families as well) there is a predictable discrepancy between, on the one hand, the profoundly painful private accounts of nativist assaults that such families endure; and on the other hand, the sanitized accounts that, in time, become part of America's master narrative. I also knew that the master narrative rarely includes the policies, laws and actions that the nation is not inclined to remember but that immigrant families are not inclined to forget.

What teacher can resist a teachable moment? What follows are several motifs that appear and reappear currently in the literature we read, the films we see, and the news we hear. In class that semester when the texts led us to a focus on contemporary nativism, I often annotated the discussion by relating my family members' experiences, hoping that my students would see that much in my family's experience resonated with theirs. Ideally, I hoped they would recognize that there is more that connects us than separates us, unlike them though I seem.

RACE, OTHER ETHNICITIES, AND IMMIGRATION

One effective strategy for rendering current immigrants as "other" is to emphasize the ways in which they are racially (or religiously) distinct from those whose families arrived in the past. Currently that distinction is made by underscoring that few immigrants come from Europe. President Trump, for instance, has openly wished for more immigrants from Norway (Libell and Porter). More recently, a Trump administration immigration official, Ken Cucinelli, implied that previous immigrants had been more welcome because they were European (Fortin). In our time there is research demonstrating that immigrants are racialized—or "re-racialized"—to make them other (Massey).

My grandparents were European, but they certainly weren't welcome, and were keenly aware of the ethnic pecking order. In family stories, when WASPs were the source of praise, they were mentioned by name—and included among ethnic groups with status were the Irish, an initially denigrated immigrant group, but one which had preceded the twentieth century immigrant wave by several decades. Mr. Petersen, over whose grocery they lived, admired my grandmother's singing voice, which he could hear as she washed the stairs to their apartment every week, so much so that he would stop whatever he was doing to listen. Miss Sollarde, the social worker in the neighborhood settlement house, praised my grandmother because her children were always so clean; Miss Loughlin thought my mother was the smartest girl in her class and saw to it that she skipped the third grade. (The sole exception to such ethnically reverential treatment was the unfortunately-named Miss Asquith, my aunts' and uncles' piano teacher, whom privately they referred to as "Miss Broadbottom.") In hindsight, I understood that they were not only conveying the existing pecking order but finding a way to bolster their own self-esteem.

Eventually, though, my family wasn't designated as white either, at least officially, a fact I readily share with incredulous students. In 1911, six years after my grandparents' arrival, an influential Republican senator from Vermont—William Dillingham, later leader of a Congressional Immigration Commission—sought to all but eliminate Southern- and Eastern-European immigrants. One of his tactics was to commission and publish (at government expense) *Dictionary of Races or Peoples* (The Immigration Commision), which explicitly re-categorized immigrants not by country of origin but by race, with a meaning not identical to race as it's used to today, but to make the case that an immigrant from an "acceptable" nation might not be acceptable because of his or her ethnicity. *The New York Times* thought the book's contention newsworthy enough to warrant a prominently placed full-page spread ("The Races That Go Into the American Melting Pot").

According to *Dictionary of Races or Peoples*, all Jews were "Hebrews" regardless of their country of origin. As for my Bongiorno grandparents, they were no longer white (as they and their countrymen had previously been described in the press) but Southern Italian, a race distinct from (and less welcome than) Northern Italian, as *The New York Times* pointed out more than occasionally ("The Races That Go Into the American Melting Pot"). Teddy Roosevelt had been elected vice president in 1900, becoming president when President William McKinley was assassinated. In November 1904, almost exactly a year before my grandparent's arrival, Roosevelt was elected president. In 1891, four years before my grandfather's first arrival, Roosevelt had been a minor government official and had followed news of the lynching of eighteen Italians in New Orleans. In a letter to his sister, Roosevelt used an ethnic slur to refer to Italian diplomats—"dago diplomats"—and characterized the lynching of these diplomats as "rather a good thing, and said so" (Iaconis).

I also tell my classes that the strategy of characterizing new immigrants as non-white did not begin with Senator Dillingham but goes as far back as 1751. That was the year that Ben Franklin, in an essay entitled "Observations Concerning the Increase of Mankind," complained about German immigrants, describing them as "swarthy," a characterization he also applied to Italians, Spaniards, the French, Russians, and Swedes. He explicitly notes that the British are one of the few "white" populations, saying, "I could wish their numbers are increased."

CRIMINALIZING THE IMMIGRANT

Another recurring strategy for designating immigrants as "other" is to brand them as criminals. The Trump administration alleges that immigrants or refugees from Honduras, Guatemala, El Salvador (and even the hurricane-devastated Bahamas) are drug dealers or connected to the gang MS13 and that Muslim immigrants from anywhere are connected to terrorism. When the Irish first arrived, the vehicle used to transport those who ran afoul of the law became known as a "paddy wagon," while the Italians were seen as violent, connected to the "Black Hand," or the Mafia, an association that lasted for decades, maintaining its association with violence while becoming increasingly sentimentalized, as in *The Sopranos*.

One of the central stories in my own family, which taught me how difficult it was for my family to be Italian in early twentieth-century America, was about the despair in my grandparents' household on the morning of August 23, 1927, when they heard on the radio that Italian immigrants Nicola Sacco and Bartolomeo Vanzetti had been executed for murders that many national and international defenders believed they did not commit (and for which they were later exonerated). Anarchists were barred from entering this country as of 1903, and both men were anarchists, but it was understood that it was antipathy to Italian immigrants that prevented them from getting a fair trial.

THE UNDOCUMENTED IMMIGRANT

Quite a few students in my class have privately—and sometimes openly—acknowledged their status as undocumented immigrants as well as the shame they felt as a result. Issues having to do with problematic legal status show up repeatedly in the immigration texts we read. More than occasionally, the issues thwarting immigration have nothing at all to do with illegal entry but with government snafus or an immigrant error. Such is the case in stories by Chimamanda Adichie, in both the fiction and nonfiction of Edwidge Danticat, and in the films *Balseros*, a documentary, and *The Visitor*, a feature.

Visas did not become a part of immigrant life until 1924, with many groups being denied visas or made ineligible for citizenship solely on the basis of race. Had my grandparents become citizens, their legal presence would have been confirmed. Barring that, proof of legal entry lay in being able to demonstrate that an immigrant was identified by name and place of origin on the manifest of the ship that they traveled on. Later, I learned that my grandfather had begun citizenship proceedings when he arrived at Ellis Island in 1895, but for whatever reason—bureaucratic snafu or my grandfather's ignorance—neither his citizenship status nor my grandmother's was revisited when he arrived again in 1905, with my grandmother as his young bride.

With the advent of World War II, the United States was at war with Italy, and so my grandmother's legal status depended on her being able to prove she had entered the country legally. My grandmother knew she had arrived at Ellis Island in November 1905, but she could not remember the exact date of her arrival nor the name of the ship she had come on. (Much much later, a great-granddaughter my grandmother didn't live to meet went searching, only to learn that "Bongiorno" had been misspelled on the ship's manifest anyhow.)

The result? Although my grandmother's entry was in fact perfectly legal, and though she had one son in the Army, another son in the

Navy, and a daughter who was a nurse in the WACS (Women's Army Corps), she nonetheless had to register as an "Enemy Alien." According to the family story, she even had to go to a government office to be fingerprinted and was given an ID card that she had to carry with her at all times.

It was a public shaming that required such residents to be fingerprinted, to register as "Enemy Aliens," to carry "Enemy Alien" identification cards, and, in some cases, to be subjected to curfews and the forced surrender of their cameras. Worst of all, they were exposed to the risk of deportation or imprisonment. We are well aware of the internment of Japanese residents from 1942 to 1946. Less well-known is that some Italians were interned from 1941 to 1942. It was a moment of profound and traumatic shame in my grandmother's life and in the family's life.

POST-MEMORY AND INTERGENERATIONAL TRANSMISSION OF TRAUMA

Well-known is Marianne Hirsch's theory of intergenerational transmission of trauma as it applied to her experience as the Romanian-born child of Ukrainian Jews who lived through World War II, though they were not themselves in concentration camps, and came to the United States when Hirsch was twelve.

I did not think, though, that Hirsch's theory applied to me. But with the growth of American nativism, especially following the US presidential election of 2016, I had an experience that made me reconsider Hirsch's theory and made me wonder whether I had too quickly agreed with my student who assumed that I was not personally affected by the rising anti-immigrant sentiment in this country. As it became increasingly clear that Trump's bias against Muslims and Latinos was gathering force, I had a dream about my grandmother. A nightmare, actually. In it she was at the end of a dark room, surrounded on either side by federal agents who were in the midst of fingerprinting her. She endured the process without resistance, but at the end, she turned to me, a look of frozen dread and resignation on her face. Then she turned away and was led out of the room by the agents into the dark, as I watched helplessly. That dream and a few others I had during that period made me wonder whether my own activism after Trump's election—tutoring immigrants pursuing citizenship, organizing a teach-in on the Trump administration's efforts to tighten rules admitting asylees and refugees and granting temporary protective status—went beyond my professional and academic interest.

I did not, of course, rush into class the following day to report my dream to my students, though eventually I did. However, my nightmare led me to wonder at my own immigrant legacy, and its durability, and to reconsider Marianne Hirsch's work on postmemory, which specifically argues that the trauma not directly in one's own experience could nevertheless be passed down the generations through a mixture of storytelling and family practices. Hirsch particularly links her theory to the Holocaust. However, the idea of intergenerational trauma connected to immigration is a motif in fiction and nonfiction by writers such Danticat, Díaz, Mukherjee and others. During that semester, I included Hirsch's theory, relating it to the authors we were reading as well as to myself.

Compatible theory put forward by Jean Laplanche (Faimberg), has indicated that trauma that is not one's own—including intergenerational trauma—could remain unconscious until the circumstances associated with the original trauma triggered it. In other words, what my nightmare told me was that, at least in theory—and unbeknownst to me—the trauma experienced by my grandmother and her children was my legacy *even a century later*, and that I could remain vulnerable to the trauma *they* experienced, especially after my research confirmed that whatever discrimination I had experienced had not been remotely as severe as theirs.

It is possible, I tell my students, that the current intensity of anti-immigration sentiment was akin to what Italians and Eastern European Jews had experienced a century ago. My family's experience in light of my recent experience has helped me understand the persistence of identity politics on a macro scale, even among those who consider themselves fully assimilated.

No one knows how long the current contentious moment will continue, but as long as my own family's immigration history and stories remain pertinent, I will continue to use them in my class for cameo roles because they allow students to develop a historical sense of waves of immigration to the United States, including what issues stay the same and what do not.

Nativism's cyclicity has led me not only to explore the past but to speculate with my students about what may await future generations. My grandparents arrived in this country as a young married couple in 1905, my mother was born a century ago, and I arrived in the mid-twentieth century. Right now, there are young immigrant parents all over the country—the twenty-first-century equivalents of my grandparents—who, if they are Latino or Muslim may be feeling the brunt of nativism, perhaps even more brutally than my antecedents did, as they face ever greater threats of deportation, incarceration, or civilian terrorism. Possibly these young immigrant parents have a native-born toddler in their household, the twenty-first-century successor to my mother, who may already be exposed to the legal animus toward immigrants and its impact on her family. In another thirty years, that baby may have a child of her own, a child of the third generation, and my twenty-first-century successor.

The past leads to the present as surely as the present leads to the future, and we are all served by having access to a reliable narrative. For some, as Edwidge Danticat has understood, the legacy that the past leaves to the present may be a nightmare. Yet not to investigate how the past informs the present is to leave us open to ersatz history: "If we refuse to do the work of creating this personal version of the past, someone else will do it for us," essayist Patricia Hampl warned in "Memory and Imagination." "That is the scary political fact." That's why writers write, that's why families tell stories, that's why truth and reconciliation committees exist, and that's why courses on ethnicity and immigration may, on occasion, be well-served by instructors who may find that their own ethnic and family history can contribute to enriching our students' understanding of immigrant and ethnic history.

WORKS CITED

"Chief Hennessy Avenged: Eleven of his Italian Assassins Lynched by a Mob." *The New York Times*, 15 Mar. 1891, pp. 1–2, https://www.nytimes.com/search?query=%22Chief+Hennessy+Avenged%3A+Eleven.

Faimberg, Haydee. "Apres-coup." *The International Journal of Psychoanalysis*, vol. 86, no. 1, 2005, pp. 1–13, https://onlinelibrary.wiley.com/doi/abs/10.1516/MDY4-GMDH-C1BW-MW8E.

Fortin, Jacey. "'Huddled Masses' in Statue of Liberty Poem are European, Trump Official Says." *The New York Times*, 14 Aug. 2019, https://www.nytimes.com/2019/08/14/us/cuccinelli-statue-liberty-poem.html.

Franklin, Benjamin. "Observations Concerning the Increase in Mankind." 1751. *Founders Online*, https://founders.archives.gov/documents/Franklin/01-04-02-0080.

Hampl, Patricia. *I Could Tell You Stories: Sojourns in the Land of Memory*. W. W. Norton & Company, 2000.

Hirsch, Marianne. *The Generation of Postmemory: Writing and Visual Culture After the Holocaust*. Columbia University Press, 2012.

Iaconis, Rosario A. "An Overdue Apology to Italian Americans." *The Wall Street Journal*, 8 Apr. 2019, https://www.wsj.com/articles/an-overdue-apology-to-italian-americans-11554761121.

The Immigration Commission. *Dictionary of Races or Peoples*. Government Printing Office, 1911, https://www.google.com/books/edition/Dictionary_of_Races_Or_Peoples/JQpgAAAAIAAJ?hl=en.

Libell, Henrik Pryser, and Catherine Porter. "From Norway to Haiti, Trump's Comments Stir Fresh Outrage." *The New York Times*. 11 Jan. 2011, https://www.nytimes.com/2018/01/11/world/trump-countries-haiti-africa.html?searchResultPosition=1.

Massey, Douglas. "The Racialization of Latinos in the United States." *The Oxford Handbook of Ethnicity, Crime and Immigration,* edited by Sandra Bucerius and Michael Tonry, Oxford University Press, 2016, https://www.oxfordhandbooks.com/view/10.1093/oxfordhb/9780199859016.001.0001/oxfordhb-9780199859016-e-002.

"The Races That Go Into the American Melting Pot." *The New York Times.* 21 May 1911, https://www.nytimes.com/search?dropmab=true&endDate=19110521&query=%22The%20Races%20that%20Go%20Into%20the%20Melting%20Pot&sort=best&startDate=19110521.

Stone, Elizabeth. *Black Sheep and Kissing Cousins: How Our Family Stories Shape Us.* Transaction Books, 2004.

Stone, Elizabeth. "It's Still Hard to Grow Up Italian," *The New York Times Sunday Magazine.* 17 Dec. 1978, pp. 22+, https://www.nytimes.com/1978/12/17/archives/its-still-hard-to-grow-up-italian-maryann-dimeglio-gerbacia.html?searchResultPosition=1.

3

IMMIGRATION STORIES FROM THE DEEP SOUTH
Stories of Bias, Discrimination, and Hope

Lilian W. Mina, with Brittany Armstrong,
Venijah Bellamy, and Paul Frick

FOREWORD

As an Egyptian immigrant in the United States, I experienced inequity and injustices as a graduate student and later as a college instructor. When I moved to the Deep South in 2016, friends and colleagues warned me that I was likely to experience more discrimination and racial biases than what I'd experienced during my time in the Midwest. I thought six years of living in this country had prepared me for what was ahead, but I couldn't have been more wrong. While my fair skin, neutral features, and advanced literacy skills saved me from severe or traumatic experiences, I couldn't help but think of the injustices less privileged immigrants encounter in the Deep South of the United States. I was particularly thinking of immigrants with darker skin tone, ethnicity-laden features, language barriers, and/or in identifiable religious clothes. Hence my decision to use my privilege and positionality as a transnational teacher-scholar to explore immigrant stories in this region, a region that has been largely neglected in immigration narratives due to the traditional focus on African American narratives and the relative recentness of diverse immigration waves to it. My goal is to outline my course design, students' research and stories of immigrants, and pedagogical suggestions for college writing professors and WPAs to build courses and curricula that are culturally sensitive and inclusive to immigrants in and outside of the university.

INTRODUCTION

At the time I was teaching my course on immigration, a video of an American diner went viral and created much controversy, frustration,

https://doi.org/10.7330/9781646421664.c003

and anger among social media patrons. In the video, a white customer appears to be scolding restaurant workers as they spoke Spanish amongst themselves. He threatened to call ICE (US Immigration and Customs Enforcement) because he assumed the workers were illegal immigrants (Karimi and Lavenson). That incident, captured by another customer on video and shared widely on social media platforms, was one episode in a long series of incidents that demonstrate an apprehensive attitude toward immigrants from different ethnicities and discrimination against them based on their skin color, language, or linguistic abilities among myriad other factors.

Like the victims of this angry diner's racial rant, immigrants of Hispanic origin seem to be a constant and easy target of discrimination across the country. Although it is not the sole reason, the recent political rhetoric may have encouraged this negative and appalling treatment of Hispanics because it falsely labels all of them "illegal" who have come to the United States to "take Americans' jobs" and to "change our language and culture." Indeed, the fear of a "Mexicanized" United States is not new and dates back to the nineteenth century when what John Havard calls the "pseudoscientific, plygeneticist views" of racial intermixture resulted in degrading non-Anglo races (1). The same period witnessed the origin of the interconnection between race and national identity. Havard explains that there was a growing fear of losing the national identity of the United States to Mexico, which was perceived then as a lesser race and an Other nation. Little has changed about the perception of immigrants from Hispanic origins, and other immigrant groups, since that period.

The situation is more complex in the Deep South of the United States, where attention has been heavily laid on the relationship and conflict between two races only: Whites and Blacks. That long and bitter history of discrimination and injustices against African Americans left next to no room in this region to think about people from other races or ethnicities. As few residents in the Deep South identified as non-Black or non-White in the past, their disparate representation posited limits on whether these people were included or excluded from the national identity (Norton as cited in Havard). In other words, the subtle presence of Hispanics and immigrants from other ethnicities did not entice academic researching of these groups of immigrants or scrutinizing the problems and hardships they experienced in this region in the past.

Writing from the vantage point of an Asian American, Ronald Takaki argues that being defined as non-white means to be labeled as "different, inferior, and unassimilable" (4). That view may be responsible for the hardships immigrants, specifically non-white immigrants, face because their mere presence and their "racial diversity" cannot be reconciled with the "Master Narrative" of whiteness and Otherness (5). Takaki explains the creation of this master narrative by looking into the education system that presents the history of Anglo-Americans as the only history worth including in school curricula. Any other history is presented in these curricula from the single angle of "the White-centered view," either of African Americans, Native Americans, or people from any other race.

After living in the state of Alabama, the heart of the Deep South of the United States, for almost two years, I was curious to learn more about immigrants' lived experiences in this area. Taking an inquiry-based approach, I designed a second-semester writing course focused on research writing skills around the theme of immigrant stories in the Deep South in spring 2018. In the rest of this chapter, I will briefly introduce the course design and students' initial understanding of immigration issues in their home state. After that, three students in this course share the narratives and research findings about immigrants in the Deep South of the United States, emphasizing their growing awareness of the injustices surrounding immigrants in this region. Our purpose is not only to contest the "Master Narrative of American History" (Takaki 4), but to remedy it with the overlooked stories of immigrants from this region. At the conclusion of the chapter, I will briefly comment on students' research findings and conclusions and discuss the pedagogical takeaway points from this rich and challenging experience my students and I had for fifteen weeks.

COURSE DESIGN

ENGL 1020 English Composition II is the second of the composition-sequence courses at Auburn University at Montgomery (AUM). It is a writing course that aims to teach students research writing skills through engaging in multiple projects centered around a specific theme. The course description offered students a point of departure to think about immigration and the stories of immigrants they may have encountered in their neighborhoods, schools, and/or workplaces (figure 3.1).

Course readings consisted mainly of two edited collections on immigration: Bob Blaisdell's *Essays on Immigration* and Richard Lingeman's *This Immigrant Nation: Perspectives on an American Dilemma: Articles from the Nation 1868–the Present*. My choice of these two books was deliberate because collectively they introduce students to the history of

This nation started, and has continued and thrived, as a nation of immigrants. From founding fathers coming from Europe, African Americans sent to this country against their will, Jewish fleeing discrimination in Europe and the Middle East, Asians escaping from different oppressive living and political conditions, to Arabs and Latinx looking for a better life for themselves and their families, the United States became to be the country we know today. Many immigrants chose to make new homes in the Deep South, a region that is largely neglected in immigration narratives due to the traditional focus on African American narratives and the relative recentness of diverse immigration to it.

In this course, we will explore, research, and understand more about these stories about immigrants in the Deep South. You may choose to focus on any of the following topics or come up with your own unique topic of interest:

- Literacy across borders
- Language barrier and learning, and monolingual ideology
- Language and nationalism
- Whiteness and color
- Re-education in the US to find jobs: time and struggle
- Foreign names and stigmatization
- Culture shock, rehabilitation, and adjustment
- Identity conflict across geographical and emotional borders
- Tolerance and inclusiveness (or lack thereof)

Figure 3.1. ENGL 1020 English Composition II course description.

immigration in the United States. Whereas Blaisdell's book contains a wide selection of essays and letters written by various immigrants about their lived experiences navigating the social, linguistic, emotional, and economical currents in the United States at the time of their arrival in the country, Lingeman's book documents the history and rhetoric of immigration using editorials from the *Nation*. My purpose of choosing these two books, in addition to a collection of online resources, was to embrace Takaki's call for more exposure to and understanding of other cultures and histories, especially of those existing in the United States. I aimed for students to learn the counter-narrative that was uniquely different from the master one they may have learned all their life through a monochrome educational system or a culture that fixated on the Blacks and Whites conflict. Therefore, my hope was for these two books to introduce students in the Deep South to an alternative narrative and rhetoric about immigration history and laws in the United States.

At the outset of the semester, I asked students about their personal experiences with immigrants they may know. It was important for me to learn about students' knowledge, experiences, and the type of narrative they have been exposed to or have developed about immigration. Many students responded that they had known immigrants either closely as family members and coworkers or remotely as neighbors. Students' responses, however, demonstrated simplistic binary conceptions: Immigrants struggle at the beginning to make their way up the social and economic ladder but they succeed and thrive after a short while, or immigrants face discrimination and prejudice because of their immigration status. What struck me in students' responses was their simple and superficial thoughts as they didn't question the reason for these struggles, or whether it was the immigrant's responsibility, or because of bias and obstacles put by the society. Interestingly, students who were immigrants themselves or had close connections to immigrants, had more sophisticated conceptions of immigration. For example, one student described the discrimination and hardship his Italian grandfather faced when he first arrived in the United States. His grandfather was labeled as dangerous by many Americans only because of his Italian roots and the fallacious generalization at the beginning of the twentieth century that Italians were gangsters and troublemakers. That prejudice against Italians made it difficult for him to get a job or to find a place to live for a long while. This student's story received comments of empathy from an immigrant student and from one who has immigrants in their family.

Another student talked about how her personal interaction with an immigrant colleague refuted all the single-narrative rhetoric about immigrants in the media and talk shows. She talked about the colleague's resilience and immaculate work ethics that not only paved his way to start his own business and to have better opportunities, but also made people who knew him rethink their preconceived prejudice against immigrants that were mostly influenced by the media and public rhetoric.

These students' stories indicated that personal experiences with immigrants were key to developing a counter-narrative or a more nuanced one from the dominating master narrative that is generally negative about immigrants, their work ethics, their lack of professional skills or knowledge, or their taking advantage of the welfare system in the United States. These early stories in the course made me think that researching immigrants' stories rather than researching immigration at large would put students face-to-face with their own prejudices and oftentimes their inadequate knowledge about immigrants.

The course included four major assignments, mimicking a typical research process: a research proposal, an annotated bibliography, a literature review, and a final research paper. I adopt a primary-research approach in my research writing courses because I'm a firm believer in the value of conducting research, small-scale as it may be, for undergraduate students. Students usually are more engaged and invested in their research topics, develop an array of transferable academic skills (e.g., thematic analysis of findings and research ethics), and they develop a strong agency as they become owner of new knowledge that they collected and generated themselves (Mina et al.).

It wasn't surprising, then, to see students choose research topics related to or inspired by the lived experiences of immigrants they have known. For example, Paul Frick and his sister are married to Latinx immigrants while Brittany Armstrong lives in a neighborhood where Korean immigrant families are the majority of residents. Not only did proximity to immigrants facilitate the primary research portion of these students' projects, but it also created a deep sense of connection, advocacy, and empathy between students and immigrants in general beyond the few in their close circles.

In the following sections, Venijah, Paul, and Brittany share a summary of their research on Hispanic and Korean immigrants in Alabama and their responses to and learning from their findings. While Venijah and Paul were curious about the role of education in Latinx immigrants' lives in the Deep South of the United States, especially in the state of Alabama, Brittany was more interested in the cultural assimilation of Korean immigrants in Montgomery.

BUILDING BRIDGES OVER LANGUAGE BARRIERS
Venijah Bellamy

Millions of immigrants come to the United States looking for more opportunities and are successfully doing so. The United States has the world's second largest Spanish-speaking community after Mexico. According to a new study published by the prestigious Instituto Cervantes, there are 41 million native Spanish speakers in the US plus a further 11.6 million who are bilingual, mainly the children of Spanish-speaking immigrants. This puts the US ahead of Colombia (48 million) and Spain (46 million) and second only to Mexico. (Burgen)

This creates a big shift in the United States demographics, transforming many areas all over America, the South being a huge area impacted. I chose to research immigration in terms of language barriers among Hispanic immigrant students in high schools in the Deep South. My goal of this research was to learn about the disadvantages that Hispanic immigrant high school students face in Southern US school systems due to these language barriers. I wanted to learn how educators can help immigrant students in their academic development, and how schools in the Deep South can bridge the differences concerning immigrants' culture and language. Education is a key factor for success and taking the steps to correct issues in the educational system can benefit immigrants and help them build a better future.

For my research I wanted to focus on two factors: bilingual education and student-teacher relationships in Southern school systems. I gathered my data through conducting a survey in Montgomery, Alabama at AUM and Park Crossing High School.

BILINGUAL EDUCATION

My first question was about implementing bilingual education into the Southern school system curriculum. From the results of my survey, a majority of my participants (67%) were in favor of implementing bilingual education into their school system while only 11 percent of participants were opposed to the idea. Another question in my survey was about whether bilingual education separates students or brings them together by means of inclusivity. Ten of my participants (about 56%) felt that bilingual education helps bring students together, while five of my participants were neutral and three participants felt that bilingual education would not bring students together. Participants didn't offer any reasons why they thought this way.

These results show that implementing bilingual education into Southern school systems is up for demand. This confirms Eugene Garcia and Bryant Jensen's similar findings in their research study "Helping Young Hispanic Learners," inferring how bilingual education and dual language programs can support Hispanic students with better literacy development in English. The study also brought forth the idea of how integrating English and Spanish speakers into the same classroom brings ethnic and linguistic equity, combating any animosity of negative attitudes that stem from discrimination against Hispanic students in the school system. South Carolina, Alabama, and Tennessee had the fastest growing foreign-born populations during the 2000s, changing the Southern States as a whole. Due to huge demographic change of the population, it is ideal for these Southern school systems to expand their development in necessary training and new ways of teaching. A huge problem facing Latino/Hispanic immigrant students in the South is the lack of instructors that are trained in bilingual education or ESL methodology, a topic worthy of further research.

STUDENT-TEACHER RELATIONSHIPS

The last survey question focused on the significance of student–teacher relationships. The answers once again were surprising, with only 39 percent choosing yes, 29 percent choosing no, and 33 percent being neutral. Looking deeper and cross-tabulating answers, I found that a majority of my participants who answered positively were immigrant participants and those who answered no were nonimmigrant ones. A majority of the immigrants I talked to while completing the survey said that they felt disconnected with their teachers, who had no understanding of their cultural background and language. Inadequate and weak relationships between Hispanic students and teachers threaten and reduce students' success in their academic career.

Discussion

How can Southern US education systems help bridge the gap that language barriers bring upon Hispanic immigrant high school students in their school system? In his study, David Becerra presented barriers that lead to Latino/Hispanic students not performing as well as their white peers, one of which is that "[w]hite teachers don't understand Latino culture" (172). Moreover, Barbara Schneider, Sylvia Martinez, and Ann Owens introduced how academic success in the classroom relies on a student's ability to view their teacher as trustworthy, whether it be through a bond of cultural understanding or "internalized sense of belonging" in the classroom (198). These findings show just how essential it is for immigrant students to have a connection with their instructors in order to navigate a different education system and to succeed. Not only do these results answer my research question, but they also suggest that

Southern US education systems can help bridge the gap in their school systems by hiring more teachers that have Hispanic backgrounds or by training teachers to become more aware of their students' cultural background and language.

Overall my research has helped me learn how schools in the Deep South can work to bridge the gaps that language barriers have brought to their school systems. I learned how important it is for immigrant students to have a connection with their instructors on a cultural level as well as how vital it is for school administration and staff to reach out to parents to help their students' academic success. The influx of new immigrants bringing in a different culture and alternative language since the beginning of the twenty-first century has created a demographic shift in the Deep South of the United States, causing a need for implementing bilingual education into Southern school systems, a demand for more Hispanic instructors, and proper communication of school staff with Hispanic families with children in the US public school system due to language barriers. Fairness and equity require schools to do more to help immigrant students succeed as well as their native counterparts.

LATINOS IN THE DEEP SOUTH: HOW WELCOME ARE THEY?

Paul Frick

Having been born in Mexico City, Mexico and raised in Miami, Florida and married to a Latina, I feel that I am uniquely positioned here in the Deep South. I wanted to look into what kind of welcome Latino immigrants in the Deep South receive and how that is affected by their native language and English linguistic competence. I decided to conduct interviews to gain a better understanding of how Latinos are treated here in the Deep South and to see how language is a major factor in the equation. I interviewed two individuals, both are middle-aged Latinos closely tied with the Latino community in Opelika, AL.

The bulk of my first interviewee's formal education took place in Mexico prior to his immigration. Prior to moving to the United States, he took a six-month English course in Mexico to help him prepare. Even with this course he found that he was unable to understand anything his boss was saying and recounted how difficult it was in the beginning. For the first month, he was very frustrated and said he "had to start from zero." The Southern accent was what made it so difficult for him to understand, but his persistence and his boss's patience helped the process along. He was able to take free English classes at a local church, where he was encouraged by the teacher. Being able to read and write in Spanish and having been educated prior to immigrating was an asset in his transition.

My second interviewee said that the process of reopening a restaurant after her parents had purchased it from her uncle went smoothly, stating, "as long as you have what you need the process goes smoothly." She shared that when her parents were purchasing the restaurant, the fact that her mother is bilingual was extremely helpful and that she was able to confidently speak up and communicate well and without reservation. However, things could be different for immigrants who are not bilingual.

DISCUSSION

One thing that my first interviewee credits with being able to make a decent transition here in the Deep South is his education. Clearly it was not the six-month course that left him frustrated upon arrival and starting "from zero." Looked at within context, he was referring to a term *bien educado* used among Latinos to denote one's upbringing at home. This is a process in which families impart manners and customs to children. From table manners to communication emphasizing respect and politeness, many Latinos value their children being "well educated," which is the direct translation of *bien educado*. It is not something that happens in a classroom but at home. He says that this is what makes a big difference in how someone is received by others, especially when they are a newcomer with a language barrier.

Because I was only able to interview two individuals, my findings are limited. There are some new ideas, but these are not comprehensive or conclusive. The welcome that Latino immigrants are receiving in the Deep South is quite variable and seems to be shaped by a variety of things including education, language, and attitude. Language differences create the most significant cultural chasm between immigrants and their host communities. Because my findings are specific to the Deep South, they not only support but add to what the Pew Research Center concluded: "Language is one of the key forces behind the process of assimilation of Latinos in the United States" ("Assimilation and Language"). This idea is echoed by Neal and Bohon stating that an increased volume of Spanish-speaking immigrants in Georgia has sparked a language controversy (Neal and Bohon).

CULTURE SHOCK, REHABILITATION, AND ADJUSTMENT
OF KOREAN IMMIGRANTS IN THE DEEP SOUTH
Brittany Armstrong

The broad topic of my interest is the culture shock, rehabilitation, and adjustment of Korean immigrants in the Deep South. The goal of my research was to learn about the reasons that motivated Koreans to come to the United States and, most important, the rehabilitation and transition process. The Korean immigrants I interviewed have been in the United States since 2008 and in Montgomery, specifically, since 2016.

The major themes that emerged from my findings were the reasons why Korean immigrants wanted to leave Korea and move to the Deep South of the United States, the culture shock experienced along the way, and the steps that were taken to overcome challenges during the adjustment process. Here, I'm focusing on the last two themes only.

According to one of my interviewees, the main shock was the dialect; "In Korea, when we study English, the textbook may say, 'Good morning, how are you?' Soon after coming to America, I would hear people say, 'What's up?' and I had to figure out what that meant." Then there are other shocks, such as how Americans are really vocal and opinionated, the way Americans hug, touch, and make eye contact when greeting others was a source of continuous shock and uncertainty among participants in my research. During my interviews, I learned that in Korea, people do not make eye contact, which explains the culture shock many of them experience when they communicate in the United States.

We also discussed what my interviewees did to help them and their families become adjusted to life in the United States. They did things like moving to high-volume Korean areas, joining social groups created by Koreans (e.g., "Mommy Politics"), and attending Korean churches. One interviewee said that they were a part of a group known as AKEEP (Alabama–Korea Education and Economic Partnership) that provides multicultural diversity education programs to both Korean and American students and professionals in Montgomery. Both interviewees said that these factors made them feel a sense of belonging, which has helped them tremendously to adjust in Alabama.

CONCLUSION

Overall, I learned that, like anything else in life, new things can be quite challenging, especially when one has to uproot everything they have ever learned and known to be able to have and enjoy what so many would take for granted. One suggestion I have is for schools to offer more classes on immigrants from all ethnicities. Knowledge of the cultural background of immigrants to our country elevates Americans' understanding and enhances their perception of immigrants. The more knowledge and understanding we have for one another, the more receptive we become of each other.

Commentary

Havard discusses the role of education in Americans' perception of other peoples. He argues that while Americans developed a hierarchical perception of other peoples and nations, they embraced the belief that all peoples "shared a common ability to improve morally and intellectually through education" (5). This is a prejudiced view that not only implies that other peoples have inferior moral and intellectual abilities until they are educated, but it also seems to propose a limited conception of education that could improve these abilities: American education. In her research, Venijah concluded that bilingual education and understanding immigrant students' cultural and linguistic background is likely to help them succeed in their school education, while Paul found that Americans don't seem to appreciate any other education that doesn't conform to their expectations, especially home education or education in a different language, as his participants suggested. Failing to establish a more encompassing education system and the unwillingness to acknowledge or appreciate other forms of education widens the achievement and success gap for immigrants to the Deep South because they are expected to, citing one of Paul's interviewees, "start from zero." That is to say, the rigid educational and social system sets immigrants up for failure because it requires them to disregard their education and language in exchange for earning acceptance and respect, and fair treatment.

When immigrants find themselves obliged to discard, rather than build on, their existing resources in order to be accepted in the American society, their assimilation process becomes "incidentally humiliating," as Blaisdell asserts (vi). He attributes this humiliation to two main reasons: language and social norms that may hinder many immigrants from successfully integrating into the US culture. The Korean immigrants' narratives in Brittany's research supports Blaisdell's assertion because they had to overcome a considerable amount of discomfort and apprehension as they maneuvered their way into the culture of the United States and the Deep South. However, Korean immigrants appear to be more successful in finding a foot for themselves in the Deep South thanks to their collective efforts that result in establishing their own communities. Although Brittany's research doesn't tell us much about these Koreans' assimilation, it is obvious that because Koreans don't carry the same baggage of prejudice, fear, and negative rhetoric Hispanics and other immigrant groups do, they are more likely to succeed and enjoy their life in the Deep South. Another reason might be the sympathy and empathy some Americans feel toward Koreans due to the shared history in the Korean War.

AFTERWORD: PEDAGOGICAL TAKEAWAYS

Taken together, students' research findings appear to support Takaki's call for incorporating other histories and cultures in school curriculum. He discusses and cites university programs that incorporated and mandated students to study other cultures before graduation because, as he argues, such multicultural curricula would be "more inclusive," and equally, "more accurate" (6). I believe that Mexican and other Latinx immigrants present a strong candidate for inclusion in the curriculum and for expanding the "master narrative." The proximity of their countries, the prevalence of the Spanish language, and the expansion of the Hispanic culture in the United States qualify the Hispanic history and culture to claim a bigger and more affluential position in college curriculum.

Faculty specializing in multilingualism and/or multiculturalism should step up and offer upper-level and graduate-level courses that address diversity and inclusivity. For the last three years, I've taught my Multilingual Composition course to prepare future college writing teachers to teach linguistically and culturally diverse populations of students. As students read about language differences in the writing classroom (e.g., Andrade; Guerra; Horner et al.), they develop an understanding of their role as future writing teachers in embracing diversity and promoting inclusivity in their classrooms.

In direct response to the issues raised in my students' research projects, I revised the course syllabus for the undergraduate section of my Multilingual Composition course to include an entire unit on linguistic diversity in the South. My goal was to increase students' awareness and appreciation of and sensitivity to language differences and variations immigrants bring to this region in and outside of the (higher) education system. Undergraduate students engaged in readings and researching the linguistic diversity in their respective disciplines and future career paths were astonished to learn of the rich linguistic landscape in the South though appalled at the invisibility of this richness. My hope is for graduate and undergraduate students taking my course to become agents for change and advocates for more inclusive practices in their workplaces and social domains.

Furthermore, Composition program directors and instructors are encouraged to learn more about the race and ethnicity profile of student populations at their institutions. Understanding this profile should be used as a springboard to diversify the curriculum by adding multicultural materials about the cultures, races, and ethnicities represented in the institution to course readings. Through engaging students in these cultural endeavors and discussions, all students will likely develop better comprehension of their classmates' cultures, thus moving away from stereotypes and simplistic views cultivated by the media, ignorance, and/or prejudice. For example, both American and non-Hispanic students will be able to recognize the diverse nationalities, cultures, and histories obscured in the term Hispanic or Latinx. As Havard explains, using the term Hispanicism "constructs a static, simplistic narrative regarding the nature of Hispanophone peoples" (3). Teacher training on these topics should also be integral in professional development programs to promote more inclusive teaching practices among writing instructors.

This brings me to the pedagogical lessons I've learned in this fifteen-week-long journey.

- **Readings**: Because this course focuses on research writing, it was a real challenge to sustain students' interest in the assigned readings from the aforementioned textbooks beyond the point of selecting their research topics. Students lost connection with readings that were not closely related to their topics and preferred to venture away from the textbooks to find more relevant readings as they got ready to develop their argument, analyze and synthesize sources, and create their data-gathering instruments. Although I'm still navigating possible ways to overcome this problem, one way to engage students in reading about the history of immigration laws and the lived experiences of immigrants is to ask them to select relevant chapters from textbooks that they can include in their writing in all research stages.

- **List of topics**: Providing students with a potential list of topics in the course syllabus proved to be a double-edge sword. On the one hand, some students used the list as a point of departure to choose the topics that resonated with their experiences and interests. These students took advantage of the list to be able to clearly articulate their topics early before they took these topics in more personalized directions. Unfortunately, other students insisted on treating the list as they'd do a packaged TV dinner; they assumed adopting a topic from the list would be as easy as microwaving their packaged dinner without allowing themselves to explore other "fresh" options. These students struggled the most in the course as they couldn't establish an organic relationship with their packaged topics. In future courses, I may create a list of topic words (e.g., identity, language barrier) that introduces students to broad ideas without packaging them, thus pushing students to think for themselves and select the angle that looks more engaging to them.

WORKS CITED

Andrade, Maureen Snow. "International Students in English-Speaking Universities: Adjustment Factors." *Journal of Research in International Education*, vol. 5, no. 2, 2006, pp. 131–154.

"Assimilation and Language." *Pew Research Center's Hispanic Trends Project*, 19 Mar. 2004. https://www.pewresearch.org/hispanic/2004/03/19/assimilation-and-language/.

Becerra, David. "Perceptions of Educational Barriers Affecting the Academic Achievement of Latino K-12 Students." *Children and Schools*, vol. 34, no. 3, July 2012, pp. 167–177.

Blaisdell, Bob. "Note." *Essays on Immigration*, edited by Bob Blaisdell, Dover Publications, 2013, pp. iii–ix.

Burgen, Stephen. "US Now Has More Spanish Speakers Than Spain—Only Mexico Has More." *The Guardian*, 29 June 2015, https://www.theguardian.com/us-news/2015/jun/29/us-second-biggest-spanish-speaking-country.

Garcia, Eugene E., and Bryant Jensen. "Helping Young Hispanic Learners." *Educational Leadership*, vol. 64, no. 6, 1 Mar. 2007, pp. 34–39.

Guerra, Juan C. *Language, Culture, Identity and Citizenship in College Classrooms and Communities*. Routledge and National Council of Teachers of English, 2016.

Havard, John C. *Hispanicism and Early US Literature: Spain, Mexico, Cuba, and the Origins of US National Identity*. The University of Alabama Press, 2018.

Horner, Bruce, et al. "Language Difference in Writing: Toward a Translingual Approach." *College English*, vol. 73, no. 3, 2011, pp. 303–321.

Karimi, Faith, and Eric Levenson. "Man to Spanish Speakers at New York Restaurant: 'My Next Call Is to ICE." *CNN*, 17 May 2018, https://www.cnn.com/2018/05/17/us/new-york-man-restaurant-ice-threat/index.html.

Lingeman, Richard, editor. *This Immigrant Nation: Perspectives on an American Dilemma: Articles from the Nation 1868-the Present*. The Nation, 2014.

Mina, Lilian W., et al. "Class-Based Research in the English Composition Class." *Perspectives on Undergraduate Research and Mentoring (PURM)*, vol. 3, no. 1, 2013.

Neal, Micki, and Stephanie A. Bohon. "The Dixie Diaspora: Attitudes Toward Immigrants in Georgia." *Sociological Spectrum*, vol. 23, no. 2, 2003, pp. 181–212.

Schneider, Barbara, et al. "Barriers to Educational Opportunities for Hispanics in the U.S." *Hispanics and the Future of America*, edited by Marta Tienda, National Academies Press, 2006, pp. 179–122.

Takaki, Ronald. *A Different Mirror: A History of Multicultural America*. Back Bay Books/Little, Brown and Company, 2008.

PART 2

Teaching through the Stories

4

REORIENTING VIA TRIAD
From Animals, Rapists, and Gang Members to Living, Breathing, Human Beings

Katie Daily

We live in a nation, and under an administration, that is increasingly concerned with the role of immigrants in America. Since 9/11, discussions of immigration and immigrants have become intertwined with criminality: terrorism, gang violence, and more, all under the umbrella term "illegal." Whereas actions are legal or illegal, political rhetoric in America has come to refer to people as "illegal," leaving us, as American citizens and consumers of literature and rhetoric, to unpack the incredibly complicated language and connotations surrounding contemporary immigration policies and narratives. As educators, how do we guide our students through the contentious issues surrounding immigration without classroom discussions devolving into unproductive political sparring matches? How do we encourage an examination of rhetoric rather than refereeing standoffs of personal beliefs? As Miguel Vasquez explains, we as educators "have a unique opportunity to help students develop the civic skills that will enable them to operate in and contribute to the modern globalized world" (par. 3). We must move toward discussions of immigration reform that are productive, nuanced, and allow for diverse viewpoints, highlighting the usefulness of approaching immigrant stories from multiple angles with an eye toward social justice and action.

This essay proposes a pedagogical approach to a triad of texts that are useful for orienting students to the language of immigration so that they can engage more thoroughly and intelligently in discussions of justice and equity in relation to America's immigration system. The classroom lesson sequence proceeds as follows: I suggest a brief examination of the term "illegal" as it applies to human beings, a concise explanation of the Department of Homeland Security and Immigration and Customs Enforcement (better known as ICE), and then an extended discussion of three texts by Edwidge Danticat: *Brother I'm Dying* (a full-length

https://doi.org/10.7330/9781646421664.c004

memoir), "Hearing on Detention and Removal" (a written testimony submitted to the House Judiciary Committee), and "Poetry in a Time of Protest" (a *New Yorker* social commentary). Students come away educated. None are indifferent. Some are enraged. All of them are deeply considering the ethical implications of immigration policies in contemporary America.

In the pages that follow, I discuss one successful approach to teaching the writings of Edwidge Danticat in four-year college composition and literature settings. Specifically, I teach three Danticat texts, all on the same subject, as a way for students to begin to grasp the rhetorical opportunities available for engaging with public discourse surrounding immigration justice, policies, and reform. This has been particularly interesting, pedagogically speaking, while teaching at the United States Military Academy (West Point) given how this particular population of students will inevitably grapple with justice and equity in our world as they emerge from their undergraduate education as officers in the United States Army. Engaging with Danticat's narratives not only promotes a discussion of policy and reform through her writing rather than our opinions, but it also allows students to tell their own stories, since many West Point cadets are either immigrants themselves (naturalized citizens) or first-generation Americans. Much like the pedagogical work of Margaret M. Chin at Hunter College, this connection between the texts and personal histories helps "students appreciate the complexities of contemporary immigration. . . . They learn to discuss immigration policy more thoughtfully and ultimately become more reflective participants in society" (par. 2). At West Point, each young adult who takes the oath to become a cadet has thought, either briefly or deeply, about their identity as an American citizen. The sharing of their family histories and personal anecdotes allows for a widening of the class's views on immigration in America. As Patricia Enciso demonstrated in her 2011 study of immigration storytelling, "stories told among peers have tremendous potential to engage students in sustained social critique" (21), which is the goal of Danticat texts. This shared engagement allows them to tell stories, listen critically, and think about the space that they inhabit within the American collective.

At West Point, the ~4,400 members of the Corps of Cadets spend four years earning their Bachelor's of Science degree in a liberal arts discipline before commissioning as Second Lieutenants (officers) in the United States Army. As young men and women, the cadets are expected to perform well academically while also becoming leaders of character through their military curriculum. All cadets coming through West

Point enroll in both EN101 (college composition) and EN102 (studies in literature). In EN102, we continue the work of EN101, layering on complex rhetorical situations and pushing our students to think broadly about literature. It is in this course that we have the opportunity to encourage these future Army officers to think deeply about the world they are about to enter and the nation they will swear to defend. Particular to writing, West Point's stated goal is to "provide Cadets with continuity and coherence in their education so that all graduates are thoughtful, agile, and clear communicators prepared to answer the various demands of their professional environments and succeed as Army officers" ("Mission"). In this context, it is a natural fit to teach immigration narratives with an eye toward social justice and equity. Danticat's triad of texts fits easily into this rubric, giving the opportunity to examine the story of her uncle Joseph through three different non-fiction genres: memoir, expert testimony, and social commentary. This navigation of multiple genres promotes intellectual agility as a transferrable skill for young men and women who will be communicating up and down a hierarchical chain of command that demands an ability to traverse genres and audiences with natural fluency.

Before diving into Danticat's texts as a rhetorical lens for immigration and justice, we must first re-humanize immigrants for our students. Immigrants are not "animals" (Davis) or "illegal" (Hawkins), which are terms often bantered about (with disturbing ease) by politicians, in the media, and surrounding discussions regarding immigration. We cannot, as educated citizens, talk about our fellow humans as if they are less-than. As Elie Wiesel, the Holocaust survivor and Nobel Peace Prize winner aptly reminds us, "You, who are so-called illegal aliens, must know that no human being is illegal. That is a contradiction in terms. Human beings can be beautiful or more beautiful, they can be fat or skinny, they can be right or wrong, but illegal? How can a human being be illegal?" (qtd. in Hing et al. 158). In addition to the human element of rhetorical discourse, is also useful for students to understand that the journalism community is moving away from the term "illegal" when describing undocumented migrants. In 2013, the Associated Press announced that it "no longer sanctions the term 'illegal immigrant' or the use of 'illegal' to describe a person. . . . 'Illegal' should describe only an action, such as living in or immigrating to a country illegally" (Carroll qtd. in Colford). Once students are grounded in the necessary language to have discussions about contemporary immigration, they are ready to move into a brief history of the government agencies and policies that process immigrants and asylum-seekers in the United States.

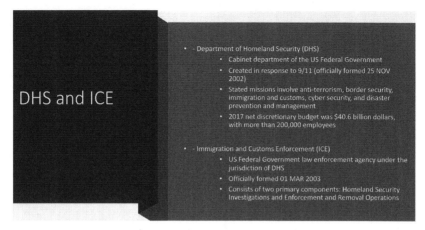

Figure 4.1. A simple PPT slide that outlines the features of DHS and ICE.

A brief (roughly forty-five minute) presentation on the Department of Homeland Security and Immigrations and Customs Enforcement is often plenty to position literature and composition students for a discussion of immigration rhetoric and social justice. Providing a simple breakdown (figure 4.1) of the agencies involved as well as a flowchart (figure 4.2) of the deportation/removal process allows students access to a useable text that is easily referenced as discussions advance. While learning about the different hearings (Bond, Master, and Merits) associated with the removal process, students come to understand the concept of "mandatory detention," which is the detainment of "non-citizens pending their immigration proceedings" (ACLU) and is often indefinite. According to a 2018 ruling by the Supreme Court, "immigrants, even those with permanent legal status and asylum seekers, do not have the right to periodic bond hearings" (Montanaro et al. 1), which equates to being held in immigration detention indefinitely while they wait for their single bond hearing. It is also important to allow students to engage with reports of conditions connected to immigration detention, since detention and the treatment of detainees is at the center of the texts in the Danticat triad. The ACLU, in their "Analysis of Immigration Detention Policies," writes that "detainees held in prisons and jails are subjected to inhumane living conditions such as inadequate and poor nourishment, lack of clothing, and overcrowding and that correctional officers often lack the language skills necessary to meet special needs of immigrants" (2).

Once students are versed in the language and systems surrounding immigration in the United States, they are ready to move to the texts.

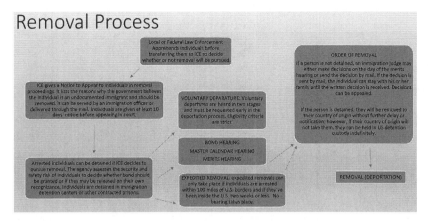

Figure 4.2. A PPT slide detailing the deportation/removal process.

The reasons for giving a background in linguistic choices and the immigration system are so that students are ready to discuss justice and equity as it pertains to human beings, not the amorphous idea of "illegal immigrants" that resides in contemporary rhetoric. When the idea of immigration is re-humanized, when our students understand that we are discussing human lives and fates rather than "animals," they are ready to think in terms of justice, equality, and rhetorical choices. They are ready to begin engaging with Edwidge Danticat's triad of texts.

We begin with Danticat's *Brother I'm Dying*, the 2007 memoir that tells the story of her uncle Joseph Dantica's life and the tragedy of his death while being confined at the Krome Detention Center in Miami. She explains,

> I write these things now, some as I witnessed them and today remember them, others from official documents, as well as the borrowed recollections of family members. But the gist of them was told to me over the years, in part by my uncle Joseph, in part by my father. . . . This is an attempt at cohesiveness, and at re-creating a few wondrous and terrible months when their lives and mine intersected in startling ways, forcing me to look forward and back at the same time. I am writing this only because they can't. (*Brother* 26)

The notion of looking forward and back at the same time informs how we move ahead in the Danticat triad. As students engage with Danticat's writing and her uncle Joseph's story, they refer back and forward between the different narratives, exploring the ways in which she tells the same story in very different ways, for exceptionally disparate audiences. Within this unit, we focus on the rhetorical opportunities provided by the memoir form, discussing language, point of view, and emotional engagement.

As part of this first third of the triad, we also study the privatization of detention centers in the United States as well as considering Guantanamo Bay as a contested space for justice. For example, students learn that the United States runs the largest immigration detention system in the world, under the leadership of the Immigrations and Customs Enforcement (ICE) arm of the Department of Homeland Security ("Immigration and Customs"). The Department of Homeland Security is responsible for enforcing the Immigration and Nationality Act as well as investigating security issues that range from human rights and human smuggling to international cultural property and antiquities crimes ("Homeland Security"). At this point in the literary investigation, students begin to engage with justice and equity, thinking critically about law enforcement, the privatization of immigration detention, and the problematic range of Homeland Security Investigations. In spring 2018, a student (names of all cadets cited in this essay have been changed for privacy purposes) mused, with exasperation, "How can one agency *possibly* deal with human trafficking as well as someone stealing a cultural artifact?!?" (Dixon).

In addition, students learn that in 2017, the United States detained a total of 367,861 ("United States Immigration Detention") immigration and asylum seekers. In 2016, the United States expelled a total of 446,223 persons on the grounds of the immigration process ("United States Immigration Detention"). These staggering numbers help students contextualize the scope of the United States immigration detention system while they comprehensively explore Joseph Dantica's story through Danticat's writings. While we are learning about a massive system that affects the lives of millions of people, the students experience the death of one immigrant (Uncle Joseph) in painstaking detail:

> My uncle arrived in the emergency room at Jackson Memorial Hospital around 1:00 p.m. with an intravenous drip in progress. He was evaluated by a nurse practitioner at 1:10 p.m. At 2:00 p.m., he signed, in an apparently firm hand, a patient consent form. . . . At 3:24 p.m., blood and urine samples were taken. . . . At 4:00 p.m., during a more thorough evaluation . . . he complained of acute abdominal pain, nausea, and loss of appetite. . . . At 5:00 p.m., he was transferred to the hospital's prison area, Ward D . . . he was seen by a physician for the first time at 1:00 p.m. [the next day] . . . at 7:00 p.m., after more than twenty hours of no food, he complained of weakness . . . at 7:55 p.m. his heart rate rose again and an electrocardiogram was performed at 8:16 p.m. . . . the next note shows he was found pulseless and unresponsive by an immigration guard at 8:30 p.m. . . . he was pronounced dead at 8:46 p.m. (*Brother* 237–239)

Students come to understand that Danticat received this information through the Freedom of Information Act, which allows for access to otherwise classified documents by family members or other certified recipients. At this point, it is clear to students that Joseph Dantica experienced tremendous discomfort and unjust treatment in his final days, both at the hands of Immigration and Customs Enforcement policies. After completing the story, students often want to spend time discussing their families and experiences.

It is as we transition away from the full-length memoir, reaching the climax of Uncle Joseph's emotionally-charged story for the first time, that students freely share their family narratives and experiences. In 2017, a cadet whose family emigrated from the Dominican Republic shared the story of his grandfather's struggle with warring factions between Haiti and the Dominican Republic, which led him to immigrate to Florida (Jones). Students asked questions, integrated Danticat's story into this narrative, and came to imagine what immigration looked like from a family perspective because they were able to engage a peer's individual history into the discussion. This no longer became about Joseph Dantica or statistics without faces, transitioning instead to a peer-to-peer discussion of personal experience. As many scholars have argued, "when youth have the opportunity to explain and expand on the images, emotions, and meaning of their lives, they may be recognized in new ways as people with complex social histories and insights about equity and justice" (Enciso 21).

After immersing ourselves in Dantica's story and exploring relevant history and government agencies, we move to the next piece of nonfiction: Danticat's written testimony on Immigration Detainee Medical Care, penned for the House Immigration Committee's Subcommittee on Hearing Detention and Removal. Danticat's testimony is valuable because "being asked to testify before a congressional committee is an indication that the people who make our laws believe that the information and views being presented are authoritative and provide valuable perspective on national issues" (Federation for American Immigration Reform). This unit gives the students insight into how Danticat seeks political justice for her immigrant uncle's death through a different form of nonfiction. Studying the hearing testimony not only gives students another view of the way that Danticat constructs Dantica's story, but it introduces students to the judicial process of policymaking. This awareness helps them to further develop their individual views on immigration policy and how these policies, and alterations to them, create ripple effects on American social, economic, and political life.

Similar to *Brother I'm Dying*, Danticat's hearing testimony begins with evoking the memory of her uncle:

> I write today not in my own name, but in the name—and stead—of a
> loved one who died while in the custody of the Department of Homeland
> Security and Immigration and Customs Enforcement officials, at the
> Krome Detention Center in Miami. His name was Joseph Nosius Dantica
> and he was 81 years old. He was a father of two and grandfather of fifteen,
> an uncle to nearly two dozen of us, a brother, a friend, and even, after
> surviving throat cancer, which took away his voice, a minister to a small
> flock in Port-au-Prince, Haiti. ("Hearing" 1)

What Danticat does here is masterfully condense multiple chapters
of *Brother I'm Dying* into a single paragraph. As one student pointed out
in 2017, "Ma'am, this is interesting because there's no time for Uncle
Joseph's story to unfold. Danticat has to move right to the point. She
has to shock the House Committee with his death." This sentiment of
"shock" and the condensed rhetoric employed by Danticat in this shorter
piece of writing runs through most students who experience Joseph's
story through the triad. As another observed, "Each time she tells the
story, it gets shorter, so it's interesting to see how she fits an entire life
into a few sentences instead of a few hundred pages" (Johnson).

Regarding Joseph Dantica's illness and subsequent death, Danticat
writes that Uncle Joseph's medications were taken away in "accordance
with the facility's regulations" (3).

> On the morning of his credible fear hearing, [Dantica] became ill as a
> result of this . . . he appeared to be having a seizure and he began to vomit.
> Vomit shot out of his mouth, nose, as well as the tracheotomy hole he had
> in his neck as a result of [his] throat cancer operation. . . . When a medic
> arrived, [he] accused my uncle of faking his illness. To prove his point, the
> medic grabbed my uncle's head and moved it up and down. It was rigid
> rather than limp, he said. ("Hearing" 2–3)

This portion of the narrative is taken directly from transcripts that Danticat received regarding her uncle's treatment while in ICE custody at
Krome. She chooses to insert the transcript information verbatim into
both *Brother I'm Dying* and her hearing testimony. Students often have
an a-ha moment when making this connection, noting how differently
the same sentences read when they're part of a long-form memoir versus
a shorter official document. In *Brother I'm Dying*, Joseph's death comes
after 237 pages of emotionally-engaging family memoir. In the hearing
document, it comes in the second sentence; however, as students comment, it is not any less tragic or poignant. The call for justice and reform
rings out from Danticat's writing, no matter the format. It just happens
to ring out in different ways.

Between *Brother I'm Dying* and her testimony, Danticat's explicit aims
develop and change. She transitions from telling a story to making a

case for the need to overhaul the medical system currently in place for immigration detainees. She writes, "My uncle and many of the others who have died, and are dying in the custody of the Department of Homeland Security and ICE officials did not violate any immigration laws. All many of them have done, was request asylum, which is an internationally acknowledged human right" ("Hearing" 5). Danticat continues, "They are called detainees, but really they are prisoners. As family members we quickly learn that. But even prisoners deserve to be treated fairly and decently and humanely. This is what we tell jailers of other countries. How about we practice some of it here ourselves?" ("Hearing" 6). This final statement, posited as a question, is a call to action. Rather than relying on the rhetoric of memoir in *Brother I'm Dying*, Danticat activates Uncle Joseph's story to move the readers to action, to plead for an overhaul of medical conditions and treatment of immigration detainees.

On May 25, 2018, I received the following email from a student:

> Ma'am, I'm on summer leave, but I had to take a minute to write to you. I've been following the news and watching how the Trump administration is choosing to handle immigrant families. Specifically, how they are separating caregivers and children. I thought about the images of detention centers that we looked at in class. And I thought a lot about Danticat and how she is probably losing her mind over this. I think it was in her testimony, but she asked a question about practicing what we preach, and we need to be doing that. If another country separated families like this, soldiers such as myself and my peers would be sent to intervene. Ma'am, I think we need to do better. (Smith)

Danticat's call to action in her testimony activated the thinking of a young man who read her texts in 2017 but was still thinking about them in 2018. This is the goal of Danticat's triad: activating the minds and awareness of young Americans.

After completing Danticat's hearing testimony, we read "Poetry in a Time of Protest" from the January 31, 2017, *New Yorker*, which again tells Dantica's story, but utilizing the most condensed framework for his tragic outcome. This article was written shortly after President Trump took office and is therefore within the framework of the Trump administration. Given that immigration issues continue to unfold as we teach these texts, it is also possible to add Op-Eds and other writings from popular publications as they continue to be published, all within the scaffold of the issues that Danticat discusses: detention centers, detainee medical treatment, and human rights.

She invokes Uncle Joseph yet again, but this time in a single sentence, explaining how he sought asylum and that he died in the care of

Immigration and Customs Enforcement agents. "Twelve years ago, after fleeing unrest in our native Haiti, my eighty-one-year-old uncle Joseph, a cancer survivor who spoke with a voice box, died in immigration custody in [Miami]" ("Poetry" 2). Danticat continues, "As his health worsened [while in detention], he was taken to a local hospital's prison's ward, where he died shackled to a bed, five days after arriving in the United States" ("Poetry" 3). She then reiterates that we must treat immigrants as human beings with rights, not as animals or a faceless mass of intruders. This article was written shortly after President Trump began crusading for the "Muslim Travel Ban" in 2017 (United States, Executive Order). On this, Danticat writes:

> On Sunday, dozens of us rallied in front of Miami International Airport, where my uncle was first detained, to protest Trump's executive order barring all refugees, particularly those from seven predominantly Muslim countries. Since Trump's xenophobic order was issued, the potential for my family's nightmare to be repeated in the lives of other refugees and asylum seekers has increased considerably, particularly for those who are fleeing situations in which waiting even one more day can be a matter of life and death. ("Poetry" 3)

From a purely rhetorical perspective, we dive into analyzing how Danticat's language progresses. In *Brother I'm Dying*, she is mourning the loss of her uncle Joseph. In her testimony she pleads for immigration reform. And in "Poetry in a Time of Protest" she is angry. Exceptionally, unapologetically angry. And this anger, which comes from heartbreak, flows through her words, off the page, and into the students experiencing her texts. She writes that President Trump's inauguration speech was "dark, rancorous, unnuanced" and that his administration endeavors to exclude her "black and brown neighbors, friends, and family, many of whom came to America as immigrants" ("Poetry" 1), highlighting the fear of immigrants that has come to be quotidian in 2018.

As a student asked in the spring of 2018, "Can we connect immigration problems to issues of police violence? I think there are ways to solve them both since the violence comes from racism and fear in both cases" (Peterson). This comment, which has been echoed by many students over the past few years, reflects the progress explored by Jaime J. Romo and Claudia Chavez: "Power and privilege are unequivocally intertwined with race in US society. Power, inequitably distributed, is represented by time, territory, and task. Who gets the time and attention? . . . Who is an insider? . . . Who determines what's important for us to do, value, or compare to as a measure of our worth?" (149). As students begin to comprehend inequity, they are positioned to think in terms of justice. By connecting issues such as racism, xenophobia, and violence across situations, students are able to consider their role in combatting discriminatory practices and policies.

When a student recently asked whether we, as Americans, create policies that are problematic and racist, I directed her to José Jorge Mendoza, a philosopher whose work grapples with that very question. "It is common to assume that discriminatory immigration controls are simply the result of racist or ethnocentric attitudes and beliefs, but it is also the case that explicitly nondiscriminatory—and at times even anti-discriminatory—forms of immigration control can themselves be the source of social and civic ostracism (i.e., xenophobia)" (69). Since borders such as the one running between the United States and Mexico are among the most hotly contested spaces in the world in terms of immigration, the bidirectional justice concerns of immigration reform need to be at the forefront of student consciousness.

By reading the triumvirate of Danticat's texts in combination, students have a way to directly engage with the same story by the same author through three different nonfiction modes. We reflect on questions asked by Lawrence Hanley, a professor at San Francisco State University, including, "To what extent are vernacular narratives shaped by more powerful generic narratives? How do these narratives expose silences and omissions in the dominant, generic narrative? What function does the vernacular narrative seem to fulfill for its tellers?" (150). For Danticat's texts, the more generic narrative is the one that students have a cursory understanding of when coming to the classroom: We know immigration is a problem in the United States, we see stories all over the news, and some of us closely follow these issues. This generic narrative is shaped by those in positions of political power as well as the warring sides of liberal and conservative news sources. By moving to study rhetoric, or Danticat's "vernacular," students are able to leave aside their political views by focusing instead on the texts at hand. We do not ask, "Is this right or wrong?" but simply, "What is happening?" It is through their own development of understanding that students come to understand the differences between dominant, generic narratives and those that are more nuanced when explored at a deeper level. The hope is that they transition those critical reading skills to question what they hear from politicians, news sources, friends, and family.

By using Danticat's texts and the way in which they transition from mourning and pleas in 2007 to anger and calls to action in 2017, students are able to see the development of one family's experience with US immigration over the course of a decade. Given that these three pieces of nonfiction were written by an established, gifted author, they are well-told stories, which "transform the situation [how we think about immigration] and provoke the possibility of new identities, relations of power, and narrative forms and functions" (Enciso 22). In studying Danticat's narrative over the course of weeks, students are also made to grapple with the fact that "when certain communities are forced to bear a disproportionate amount of the surveying, identifying, interrogating, and apprehending that goes along with a state's immigration enforcement mechanism, the members of that community become socially and civically ostracized" (Mendoza 76). By studying three different nonfiction forms utilized by Danticat, all narratives with her uncle Joseph at the center, students come to see that those without a voice can find advocacy in others, that they need not "be subdued by people whose power comes from their institutionally authorized positions" (Beyton and Dossa 256). They discover ways to communicate key messages across genres, which will serve them well as young Army officers tasked to engage with people from subordinates to global leaders as a daily practice. The discussions we've had in the classroom, which encourage students to carefully consider the equitable distribution of the civic rights of immigrants, have been productive, nuanced, and incredibly important, highlighting the usefulness of approaching immigrant stories from multiple angles with an eye toward social justice and action. Danticat's triad of texts meets the intent of West Point to educate, train, and inspire our students to become leaders of character prepared to communicate across domains as thoughtful, articulate Army officers. Through this textual triad, students practice their skills as critical thinkers able to deeply contemplate what it means to be an American.

WORKS CITED

Alden, Edward. *The Closing of the American Border: Terrorism, Immigration, and Security Since 9/11.* Harper Perennial, 2009.

American Civil Liberties Union. "Analysis of Immigration Detention Policies." *ACLU,* 2018, https://www.aclu.org/other/analysis-immigration-detention-policies.

Beyton, June, and Parin Dossa. "Mapping Inclusive and Equitable Pedagogy: Narratives of University Educators." *Teaching Education,* vol. 14, no. 3, 2003, pp. 249–264.

Chin, Margaret M. "Teaching Immigration through Personal Connections." *Diversity & Democracy,* vol. 13, no. 1, 2010. https://www.aacu.org/publications-research/periodicals/teaching-immigration-through-personal-connections.

Colford, Paul. "'Illegal Immigrant' No More." *AP The Definitive Source,* 2 Apr. 2013, https://blog.ap.org/announcements/illegal-immigrant-no-more.

Danticat, Edwidge. *Brother, I'm Dying.* Vintage, 2008.

Danticat, Edwidge. "Hearing on Detention and Removal: Immigration Detainee Medical Care." Government Printing Office. 4 Oct. 2007. https://www.aclu.org/sites/default/files/images/asset_upload_file782_32063.pdf.

Danticat, Edwidge. "Poetry in a Time of Protest." *The New Yorker*, 31 Jan. 2017, https://www
.newyorker.com/culture/cultural-comment/poetry-in-a-time-of-protest.

Davis, Julie Hirshfeld. "Trump Rants on Unauthorized Migrants: 'These Aren't People,
These Are Animals'." *The New York Times*, 17 May 2018, p. A13.

Dixon, Jim. "EN102: Week Eight." 19 Feb. 2018. English 102, United States Military Academy at West Point.

Enciso, Patricia. "Storytelling in Critical Literary Pedagogy: Removing the Walls between
Immigrant and Non-Immigrant Youth." *English Teaching: Practice and Critique*, vol. 10,
no. 1, 2011, pp. 21–40.

Federation for American Immigration Reform. "Congressional Testimony." *FAIR*, 2006,
https://www.fairus.org/about-fair/impact/congressional-testimony.

Hanley, Lawrence. "Working-Class Cultural Studies in the University." *Class and the College
Classroom: Essays on Teaching*, edited by Robert C. Rosen, Bloomsbury Academic, 2013.

Hawkins, Derek. "The Long Struggle over What to Call 'Undocumented Migrants,' or as
Trump Said in His Order, 'Illegal Aliens'." *The Washington Post*, 9 Feb. 2017, https://
www.washingtonpost.com/news/morning-mix/wp/2017/02/09/when-trump-says
-illegals-immigrant-advocates-recoil-he-would-have-been-all-right-in-1970/.

Hing, Bill Ong, et al. *Immigration Law and Social Justice*. Wolters Kluwer, 2018.

"Homeland Security." Department of Homeland Security. 29 August 2021. https://www
.dhs.gov.

"Immigration and Customs Enforcement." Department of Homeland Security. n.d.
https://www.ice.gov.

Johnson, Alexander. "EN102: Week Four." 8 Feb. 2018. English 102, United States Military
Academy at West Point.

Jones, Katie. "EN102: Week Three." 20 Jan. 2017. English 102, United States Military
Academy at West Point.

Mendoza, José Jorge. "Discrimination and the Presumptive Rights of Immigrants." *Critical
Philosophy of Race*, vol. 2, no. 1, 2104, pp. 68–83.

"Mission." West Point Writing Program. n.d. https://westpoint.edu/academics/curricu
lum/west-point-writing-program/the-program.

Montanaro, Domenico, et al. "Supreme Court Ruling Means Immigrants Could Continue
to Be Detained Indefinitely." *National Public Radio*, 27 Feb. 2018, https://www.npr.org
/2018/02/27/589096901/supreme-court-ruling-means-immigrants-can-continue-to
-be-detained-indefinitely.

Nevins, Joseph. *Operation Gatekeeper and Beyond: The War on 'Illegals' and the Remaking of the
U.S.-Mexico Boundary*. Routledge, 2010.

Peterson, Alana. "EN102: Week Four." 6 Feb. 2018. English 102, United States Military
Academy at West Point.

Phippen, J. Weston. "What Trump Doesn't Understand About MS-13." *The Atlantic*, 26 Jun.
2017, https://www.theatlantic.com/news/archive/2017/06/trump-ms-13/528453/.

Romo, Jaime H., and Claudia Chavez. "Border Pedagogy: A Study of Preservice Teacher
Transformation." *The Educational Forum*, vol. 70, no. 2, 2006, pp. 142–153.

Smith, Jason. "What the Hell, Ma'am?" Email, 25 May 2018.

United States, Executive Office of the President [Donald Trump]. Executive Order 13769:
"Protecting the Nation From Foreign Terrorist Entry Into the United States." 1 Feb.
2017. 82 FR 8977. https://www.federalregister.gov/documents/2017/02/01/2017-022
81/protecting-the-nation-from-foreign-terrorist-entry-into-the-united-states.

"United States Immigration Detention." *Global Detention Project*, 24 Jan. 2018, https://www
.globaldetentionproject.org/countries/americas/united-states.

Vasquez, Miguel. "Teaching Students to Consider Immigration with Empathy." *Diversity
& Democracy*, vol. 13, no. 1, 2010, https://www.aacu.org/publications-research/period
icals/teaching-students-consider-immigration-empathy.

5

INITIATING A GLOBALLY INCLUSIVE UNDERGRADUATE CURRICULUM THROUGH LUIS VALDEZ'S CHICANO/A PROTEST THEATER

Danizete Martínez

INTRODUCTION

Traditionally in Chicanx literary production, the topic of social injustice and inequity functions as an expression of protest primarily within a *Chicanx* framework. In my recent experiences teaching undergraduate composition at the University of New Mexico-Valencia branch campus—a Title-V Hispanic Serving community college—I have found students making much more strident connections between the genre and the current state of politics in the United States, namely in light of President Trump's threat of rescinding the Deferred Action for Childhood Arrivals program, or DACA. Here, in an attempt to analyze immigration rhetoric in a First Year Composition course, I examine how an example of the Chicano playwright Luis Valdez's ethnic protest drama works to inform and engage undergraduate students who are both most vulnerable to present injustices against immigrants, and those sympathetic to these injustices and are curious about pursuing different avenues of political activism. As a founding member of the California-based theater collective *El Teatro Campesino*, Valdez stylized his plays in the tradition of agitation-propaganda theater, traditionally considered a highly politicized left-wing production emerging in Europe in the 1920s, where characters were often depicted as flat and polemic, and the incendiary plot intended to incite radical action. By examining how teaching a text that deliberately exploits and subverts denigrating stereotypes of Mexican Americans, my goal is to demonstrate how Valdez's play *Los Vendidos* can work to foster a deeper understanding of social justice and advocacy for the larger Latinx and immigrant population. Additionally, reflecting on students' reactions to lessons on Mexican-American theater provides a useful pedagogical lens into student writing and the

https://doi.org/10.7330/9781646421664.c005

rhetorical connections between language, literacy, culture, and identity within a framework of composition studies. Code switching is thematically central to the play in the linguistic alternation between Spanish and English; upper-, middle-, and lower-class structures; and in the play's final scene where the essential concept of humanity is ironically destabilized. Through the discursive act of writing, students essentially "decode" the stereotypes and narrow preconceptions that drive hostile attitudes toward immigrants and people of color in the United States.

OVERVIEW OF CHICANX CULTURAL PRODUCTION

Because of the rich history that surrounds the play, I first provide an overview of the history of Chicanx culture and cultural production in order to situate *Los Vendidos* within a tradition of protest in that canon. We begin by considering the debatable etymology of the term "Chicano" that has been linked to the Nahuatl language of pre-Columbian tribes for *Mexicanos* (which they pronounced "*Mesheecanos*"). Today, the term "Chicana/o" is interchangeable with Mexican American, native born American, and Americans of Mexican ancestry. As a self-identifying term, it can reflect ethnic identity, political identity, indigenous identity, linguistic identity, and class identity. Some scholars argue that the origins of Chicanx literature can be traced to the sixteenth century, particularly to the chronicle written by Spanish adventurer Álvar Núñez Cabeza de Vaca. However, Chicanx literature (and, more generally, the Chicanx identity) is usually dated to sometime after the Mexican–American War (1846–1848) and the subsequent 1848 Treaty of Guadalupe Hidalgo.

In this treaty, Mexico ceded over half of its territory—now in the US Southwest, including California, Nevada, Utah, and much of Arizona, Colorado, and New Mexico, which had all previously been part of the Spanish Empire—to its northern neighbor. In a stroke, hundreds of thousands of former Mexican citizens became US citizens. Early forms of Chicanx literature include autobiographies and memoirs/testimonials of landowners like Miguel Otero and María Amparo Ruiz (which were written in English to show their acculturation), and *corridos*, a popular narrative ballad of Mexico. Various themes featured in Mexican *corridos* are often old legends about famed criminals or heroes in the rural frontier areas of Mexico. Nineteenth-century *corridos* often narrate cultural tensions between Mexican Americans and Anglos resulting after the Mexican-American War (1846–1848). Contemporary *corridos* written within the past few decades feature more modern themes such as drug-trafficking (*narcocorridos*), migrant labor, and immigration (as demonstrated in the popular TV series based in New Mexico, *Breaking Bad*).

TRADITION OF PROTEST IN CHICANX STUDENT YOUTH GROUPS

Political activism within Chicanx communities gained traction particularly after World War II with a focus on the quality of education being offered to Latinx students in their own communities. In the late 1960s, the mobilization of global student activism motivated the East Los Angeles student walkout that occurred on March 1, 1968, with fifteen thousand Chicanx students, faculty, and community activists protesting against the discrepant academic quality for Latino students. Student groups were additionally conscientious about other issues of social injustice that included national police brutality and conflict over Vietnam. The more militant Brown Berets, along with affiliated student college organizations that originated from the 1968 walkouts organized the Chicano Moratorium in 1970 in protest of the Vietnam War. The blowouts of the 1960s can be compared to the 2006 walkouts, which were done in opposition to the Illegal Immigration Control bill and to the recent wave of marches to support DACA recipients.

Many of today's Chicanx and Latinx student youth groups emerged from this tradition established by the early movement marches and are still active in directly addressing social injustice. For instance, the historic Movimiento Estudiantil Chicanx de Aztlán (MEChA) organization that was formed in the 1960s is still operating and promoting "higher education, community engagement, political participation, culture, and history . . . seek[ing] to open the doors of higher education for our communities and strive for a society free of imperialism, racism, sexism, and homophobia" (http://www.chicanxdeaztlan.org/). For their recent 2018 conference, the University of Utah's MeCHA's chapter announced on its website that:

> MEChA de U of U has been saddened and angered by the recent political discourses and the surge of racist, anti-queer, sexist, xenophobic, islamophobic violence, both physical and emotional. We are truly inspired by the tenacity that our communities have demonstrated by continuing to fight back. We hope to celebrate and affirm our community's resilience by sharing space, connecting, dialoguing, and collectively healing. We hope that the conference provides a space to think critically and explore issues of power, history, self-identity, and how we can decolonize the toxicity we have learned to normalize in order to take action and rebuild our communities.

This deep-rooted desire to improve Mexican-American political, educational, labor, and civil rights was the impetus of the Chicano Movement, and where the term "Chicano" was once considered pejorative, it was then used to express cultural pride and was reflected through the written and visual arts produced during this era. It was also during this time that Chicanx theater emerged.

LUIS VALDEZ AND THE HISTORY OF EL TEATRO CAMPESINO

Known as the "father of Chicano theater," Luis Valdez was born in Delano, California, in 1940 to migrant workers, and at age six he was also picking crops. The experience shaped his politics and aesthetics as an English major and drama student at San Jose State University. It was at the end of his time at the university where he where he produced his first full-length play, *The Shrunken Head of Pancho Villa* (1964), which proved to be a prototype for the style of political theater he would commit himself to. Set on the verge of the Mexican-American Civil Rights Movement, the play is cast with racist stereotypes of a dysfunctional Mexican-American working-class family in a hostile Anglo-American society that includes an alcoholic father and his resigned wife; a pregnant, unmarried daughter; one *vato loco* brother; another brother suffering from PTSD; and finally the central grotesque figure of the play, the oldest brother Belarmino (Belo), a bodiless head with an insatiable appetite. Belo, who at first only seems to communicate by singing "La Cucaracha," claims to indeed be the incarnation of the Mexican Revolutionary Pancho Villa. In the introduction to the play Valdez notes:

> The play is not intended as a "realistic" interpretation of Chicano life. The symbolism emerging from the character of Belarmino influences the style of acting, scene design, make-up, etc. The play therefore contains realistic and surrealistic elements working together to achieve a transcendental expression of the social condition of La Raza in Los Estados Unidos. The set, particularly, must be "real" for what it represents; but it must also contain a cartoon quality such as that found in the satirical sketches of José Orozco or the lithographs of José Guadalupe Posada. In short, it must reflect the psychological reality of the barrio. ("Shrunken Head" 132)

The exaggerated stereotypes and absurdity of the play characterize what happens when the Chicanx subject internalizes, resists, and rejects ambiguous racial discourses. In the play, Valdez is inciting social change through the historical figure *Villa* in order to revolutionize and reorganize the positioning of Chicanas/os within the dominant socioeconomic American paradigm through protest and radical nationalism.

The grotesque in *Shrunken Head* enacts a continuity of historical memory through the metaphor of decapitation and also through very real poverty. Belarmino's dismembered representations of the historical Mexican and Mexican-American folk heroes Pancho Villa and Joaquín Murieta simultaneously signal fissures within the Chicana/o body politic, the complexities of memory, and the ambiguous constructions of myth, family, and ethnic identity. In much the same way that Daniel Venegas does in *Don Chipote*, Valdez demonstrates the radical power of the Chicana/o grotesque to subvert dominant paradigms through caricature, vernacular, bawdy humor, and plucky opposition; this becoming his signature for his future activism and career in the theater.

After graduating, Valdez spent the next few months with The San Francisco Mime Troupe, where he was introduced to agitprop theater and Italian commedia dell'arte ("comedy of the professional actors" developed in the sixteenth century). The San Francisco Mime Troupe's mission was, and is, to create and produce socially relevant theater to be performed before the broadest possible audience ("mime" is not as in a silent pantomime, but as in "mimic"). The company, whose subject matter focuses on the impact of political events on personal lives, has historically been made up of multicultural and multiracial actors with performances always free. Early avant-garde performances stemmed from the founding director R. G. Davis's introduction to commedia dell'arte that he felt contained a universal quality that appealed to a range of audience members from different socioeconomic backgrounds. According to the troupe's mission statement:

> The SFMT delights in savaging the norms of mainstream American theater, with its naturalistic values, its emphasis on personal (or at most family) psychology, its settings confined to living rooms and patios. We admire the depths reached by 20th-century realism, but we also think it sanctions social inaction. Our characters are individuals but they are also members of social classes: conscious or unconscious participants in the unending wars over land and power and wealth which drive human history. (The San Francisco Mime Troupe)

According to Valdez, it was when he discovered the troupe that he "figured if any theater could turn on the farmworker, it would be that type of theater—outside, that lively, that bawdy" (Huerta 45). Valdez's experience with the SFMT led him to explore other experimental forms of theater and protest, eventually leading him to create *El Teatro Campesino* (The Farmworkers' Theater). Valdez worked with the Mime Troupe until the Delano grape labor strike broke out in 1965. Otherwise known as the *Huelga*, the strike lasted for five years, and after forming the United Farmworkers of America, leaders César Chavez, Dolores Huerta, and Richard Chavez organized community marches and non-violent protests to bring attention to their cause. After graduating, Valdez's commitment to tackling social injustice directed toward Mexican Americans was marked by these two life-changing events: he joined Chávez's grape boycott and strike, and he created *El Teatro Campesino* that performed for migrant and striking farmworkers with the intention of educating their audience while also educating the public about their social struggles. The group was made up of both migrant workers and students who performed their fifteen-minute one-act interlingual *actos* often out of flatbed trucks on the fields where they worked, as well as in union halls.

Chicanx theater is particularly hybridized, often drawing from a wide range of traditions including Aztec ritual; Spanish and colonial drama; Mexican drama; *pastorelas* and other Church drama; *carpas* and *zarzuelas* (traveling shows) that operated in Mexico and the Southwest from the turn of the century through the 1950s; Mexican *telenovelas*; and European and Euro-American drama (Worthen 102). Such syncretism, W. B. Worthen suggests, is strategic on the part of Chicanx playwrights who reveal the intricate dynamics of identity and locate it in a specific history of ethnic and political struggle, while at the same time subverting monologic historical representations of Chicanas/os projected by the dominant culture (102). What Valdez was trying to achieve through his plays were dramatic performances that aligned with the central tenants of the Chicano Movement as well as with the direct, nonviolent action that was fundamental to the successes of the *Huelga*. And while his stylistic sense of theater was indebted to the other traditions mentioned earlier, his *teatro* was entirely unique.

The political power of Valdez's *actos* is lost without understanding the social implications of early Chicanx theater. Yolanda Broyles-Gonzalez emphasizes the radical impulse of Chicanx theatrical production and its collective aim of social improvement:

> The Teatro Campesino's militance was a direct response to the needs of the United Farm Workers' struggle from which it emerged. There was an urgent need to unionize in the struggle against the multiple abuses of agribusiness, which included large-scale pesticide poisoning of farm laborers, exploitive wages, substandard housing, child labor and no benefits. . . . The Teatro Campesino described its work within this very combative style, a style that emanated directly from an intimate relationship to the urban and rural struggles of Chicana/o communities. The performance telos involved a grounding in the community experience of the working class, in a social vision and critique. (24)

The incentive for the *actos* was in fact to satirize the injustices the farm-workers were experiencing, while at the same time shed light on their struggles and work toward improvements in their working conditions through education and activism. According to Beth Bagby who inter-viewed Valdez in 1967, the early *actos* developed out of improvisation dealt primarily with the significance of the *Huelga*, the National Farmworkers Association, and why farmworkers should join. A significant feature of the *teatro* is the bilingual dialogue and the use of signs and props. Originally, "The Teatro has been limited to an audience of either farm workers or urban strike sympathizers, but its unwritten *actos* have established dra-matic images which will last the lives of its audiences" (Bagby 72). We see similar gestures in other current forms of entertainment including such films as such as in *The Fence/La Barda* (1994), *Farmingville* (2004), *Made in L.A.* (2007), *Amreeka* (2009), *The Least of These* (2009), and *Sentenced Home* (2009). The basic *acto* can be defined as a short, improvised scene deal-ing with the experiences of its participants where a conversation between a boss and his striking worker reveals an even more complex situation involving a Chicano and the social forces around him. Indeed, in the first edition of the publication of *Actos* by Arté Público in 1971, Valdez describes their purpose as to "inspire the audience to social action. Illumi-nate specific points about social problems. Satirize the opposition. Show or hint at a solution. Express what people are thinking" (*Actos* 12).

As has been frequently noted, Valdez's inculcation of Brecht's theat-rical approach is central to the ethos of *El Teatro Campesino*. In *Chicano Agit-Prop: The Early Actos of El Teatro Campesino*, Jorge A. Huerta states, "Like Brecht, the *teatro* does not want its public lulled into complacency. By allowing the audience members to use their collective imagination, they, too, become a part of the creative spirit and can better see them-selves in these universal types" (53). Valdez explained to Paula Cizmar in a 1979 interview for *Mother Jones*: "Brecht's technique of learning plays became a very real aspect of teatro, especially when we tried to teach workers about the grape strike. People can go on strike very simply. That's the easy part. What's hard to understand is what striking involves as well as the tactics of a prolonged struggle" (52). The purpose of his theater was indeed to incite action.

This same spirit of purpose and action still aligns with how Valdez currently views his plays. At the 2013 Latina/o Theater Common's first national meeting in Boston, Noe Montez wrote of how Valdez encour-aged the artists to continue to create an inclusive American theater where Latinx artists are actively contributing to the national discourse in productive ways (23). Montez goes on to say:

If Luis Valdez's vision for a new American theatre is to come to pass, Latinx people will need to make up a significant portion of the boards, leadership structures, artists, and audiences for theatre in the 21st century. The stage is set; now it's time to meet the moment—to look outward as much as in, and to continue the developing story of the unfolding complexity of Latinx identity in the U.S. and the Americas. The new American theatre is here, and it's here to stay. (26)

Through his creative and destabilizing manipulation of the genre, Valdez offered a new mode that in effect permitted cultural exchange and social mobility.

LOS VENDIDOS IN THE CLASSROOM

Valdez's ironic appropriation of stereotypes, considered in the context of today's political reactions to immigration, racism, and inclusivity, can provide innovative opportunities to consider issues of social justice, postmulticulturalism, and marginalized voices within the classroom. When teaching *Los Vendidos* (The Sellouts), students grapple with questions about inclusion, civil rights, identity politics, social justice, and language dominance through exaggerated representations of Mexican stereotypes. The play was first performed in 1965 in a flatbed truck during the Delano Grape Strike, later to be presented in larger venues that included the Brown Beret *junta* in East Los Angeles. *Los Vendidos* takes place in "Honest Sancho's Used Mexican Lot and Mexican Curio Shop," seemingly run by Honest Sancho, a dubious car salesman type. Miss JIM-enez—the self-loathing Hispanic secretary—is scouting for a respectable Mexican-American to be "a brown face in the crowd" (47) for California's 1960s Republican administration. She is tasked with finding a "Mexican type" for Governor Reagan's administration. Specifically, somebody "Suave. Debonair. Dark. But of course, not too dark. Perhaps, beige . . . [and] hard-working" (*Los Vendidos* 41). Sancho shows her various stereotypes of Mexican models, or robots, that include Johnny *Pachuco*, the eternal ethnic scapegoat-cum-criminal; the Farmworker, who economically runs on beans and tortillas; the *Revolucionario*, the quintessential Latin lover; and finally, Eric the Mexican American, the ideal fit for the Reagan administration looking for a token employee who will not cause waves. As the secretary hands Sancho fifteen thousand dollars for the Mexican American, he begins to "malfunction," rattling off Chicano nationalistic cries in a code-switching succession: "*¡Esta gran humanidad ha dicho basta! Y se ha puesto en marcha! Viva la causa! Viva la huelga! Vivan los brown berets! Vivan los estudiantes!* Chicano power!"

(51). The other models then turn on her, and she runs away scream-ing. In the end, the robots are fifteen thousand dollars richer, and it is revealed that the real robot was actually Honest Sancho, thus leaving us to wonder: who really are the sellouts?

Reviewing the history of Chicanx activism and literary production helps to contextualize how Valdez's ironic appropriation of stereotypes can provide innovative opportunities to consider issues of discrimina-tion, immigration, and ethnic and linguistic difference in the classroom in constructive ways. After students read the play, they are asked to read Valdez's short essays "Notes on Chicano Theater" and "The Actos," and to answer the following set of questions about the play: (1) What was the main purpose of Chicanx theater? (2) Briefly describe the plot of *Los Vendidos*; list the main characters and briefly describe them. (3) What was Valdez trying to accomplish by stereotyping his characters? Was he successful in his efforts? Why or why not? (4) Who is/are "the sell-outs" in the play and why? (5) How does language, both Spanish and English, function in the play? And (6), Is this type of theater still needed today? In general, students have no problem identifying the purpose of Chicanx theater and describing the plot. However, they do struggle with describing the main characters and Valdez's motives for his exag-gerated stereotyping. I see this, in part, when students are worried about appearing guilty of stereotyping, or even appearing racist themselves. To help them through this, I ask students to pose a general question about the play on our discussion board on our Learning Management System. Students are asked to directly respond to that question, and then respond to two classmates' posts. In their responses, students grap-ple with the notion of "selling out" and what it means to be a cultural sellout given the current incendiary rhetoric about race and difference stemming from Trump's administration. When summarizing the plots, they have no difficulties describing the play's essential plot noting the objectification and dehumanization of Mexicans as tools; however, there are differences in whom they identify as the authentic "sellouts," some calling out both Honest Sancho and Ms. Jimenez for "selling out" their culture: the secretary in her adamant rejection of her Mexican ethnicity, and the salesmen in his literal role as a Mexican vendor willing to sell his own people for profit.

In Ruben Navarette's reflection on the Hispanic internalization of the term "sellouts," he makes sense of the play's conclusion by surmis-ing: "Sancho, it turns out, is a robot and the whole thing is a scam—one that takes full advantage of popular assumptions about what kinds of Hispanics are, and aren't, acceptable. The moral to the story: It's silly to make too much of societal pressure to assimilate, just as it's silly for some people to put a higher premium on those who have assimilated than those who haven't" (Navarrette 15). However, when the topic of assimilation is being considered in today's wider and contentious discussion of immigration status, the notion of "blending in" is complicated by the questions of blending in *where* and *with whom*.

Valdez's play takes an ironic position on the assimilation paradigm and allows for the opportunity, through humor, to consider what is truly at stake when individuals from ethnic minorities are subject to deportation and/or violence namely for being the other. According to Julie Bolt, "While reading, enacting, and discussing [Valdez's] plays, students—many of them children of Diasporas—are quick to recognize nationalistic discourse on immigration and the dehumanizing rhetoric of globalization. Often, they will share stories of what they or their parents endured, not as Chicanos, but as Latinos, West Indians, African Americans, and West Africans, to name a few" (71). *Los Vendidos* addresses issues of justice and equity that emerge through the telling, writing, and remembering of the immigrant story in the writing classroom not just for a Mexican-American audience, but for many students with similar stories to tell, and for those who are concerned about any individuals who are experiencing trauma because of their heritage. Bolt notes that "[t]hrough Valdez's examples of satire and agit-prop, students address and challenge collective cultural consciousness—and themselves become agents of change" (73). Additionally, it is through satire that students are more comfortable to address the themes of individual, cultural, and systemic forms of racism that very much shape all of our daily lives.

When discussing the concept of "selling out," questions emerge about the practice of code-switching between Spanish and English, and, germane to our interests in this collection, how we navigate code-switching in the First Year Composition classroom. Code-switching transpires when multilingual speakers replace a word in one language for a word in another language, typically following similar grammatical rules (Heredia and Brown). For instance, we see this when Sancho is attempting to sell Johnny (the *pachuco* model) to Ms. Jimenez as he praises both the robot's ability to be bilingual while also suffering from an inferiority complex. To demonstrate, Johnny challenges Sancho by stating, "You think you're better than me, huh, *ese*?" (45), while swinging a switchblade. The stereotyping of Johnny as the *pachuco* scapegoat aligns with traditional linguistic interpretations of code-switching that suggests it is an act to "compensate for diminished language proficiency" (Heredia and Brown). In the case of Johnny, he is stereotypical of a Mexican American struggling between different cultures and languages, unable to feel confident in either. Code-switching between Spanish and English is extremely common in New Mexico in earnest and in jest, so my students enjoy sharing their own examples with the class (some might be familiar with Lauren Poole's delightful *YouTube* series "*Shit Burqueños Say,*" which features humorous depictions of well-known New Mexican colloquialisms). Most of the class agrees that in a cultural context, the act of code-switching exhibits cultural pride. Yet, when asked how the same act transpires in college writing, the consensus is divided. To provide a basic introduction to the linguistic study of code-switching, I refer the class to Roberto R. Heredia's and Jeffrey M. Brown's summary that considers a bilingual learner's language experience. They surmise that:

> In short, code-switching may be indicative of difficulties in retrieval (access) affected by a combination of closely-related factors such as language use (i.e., how often the first-language is used) and word frequency (i.e., how much a particular word is used in the language). Finally, the notion that people code-switch as a strategy in order to be better understood and to enhance the listeners' comprehension is another plausible alternative.

When considering teaching justice and equity through the immigrant story, it is unavoidable to reflect on how language dominance emerges in a composition classroom, particularly when a considerable number of students are native Spanish speakers who use the language to communicate with their families. First generation bilingual students bring a wealth of linguistic experiences to the FYC space, and Heredia's and Brown's suggestion of understanding code-switching as an alternative to enhance both the instructor's and the entire class's understanding of the bilingual learner posits emergent possibilities about how to approach rhetoric and writing.

Indeed, a refreshing trend in composition studies is to value the social significance of code-switching and multilingualism. In Ofelia García and Li Wei's study *Translanguaging: Language, Bilingualism and Education,* the authors carefully consider the process of translanguaging—a method in which language learners switch from first to second languages—and the benefits it can bring to current practices of bilingualism and bilingual education. By pointing out that bilingualism, mutilingualism, and plurilingualism have traditionally been conceptualized as two or more autonomous language systems, the authors suggest that a poststructuralist approach to language, one that views language as fluid and dynamic rather than static, sets the groundwork for a translanguaging approach that can transform the concept of bilingualism. While current bilingual education systems privilege a bifurcated paradigm, García and Li Wei convincingly argue that translanguaging in primary and secondary classrooms is a successful multimodal approach for language learners to weave their home language into their new language, as opposed to polarizing the two. In other words, the process of translanguaging is more attuned to the cultural hybridity contingent with our increasing globalization, and actively works to destabilize language hierarchies (69).

Both admit to the very real challenge of persuading educational authorities to accept translanguaging as a legitimate asset for students. As is the case, most resistance concerns assessment and standardized testing in primary and secondary schools. García and Li Wei astutely point out that state schools continue to insist on monolingual "academic standard" practices (47). Instead of standardized tests that are only offered in English in the United States, the authors argue for a performance and formative based Dynamic Assessment that would measure creativity and criticality. Instead of assuming the traditional role of leader, translanguaging teachers act more as facilitators and endeavor to learn along with their students. This is one of the many differences from traditional bilingual education that the authors succinctly identify. In their conclusion, García and Li Wei re-emphasize the potential of translanguaging to transform the sociopolical order by creating a space—or opportunity—for bilingual students to honor their histories, identities, heritages and ideologies (137). While the framework still needs to be fleshed out, García and Li Wei effectively argue that translanguaging is clearly a process that advocates for polymorphous language learners and is indeed worth serious consideration in our current educational system, and something worth considering in higher education curriculum, namely in two-year institutions where bilingualism and the question of how to best serve these learners is significant to say the least.

Ways that we as educators can help students explore their individual linguistic variances is by having them reflect on their personal language journeys through literacy narratives. Using *Los Vendidos* as an entry point to discuss the immigrant experience, the topic of language learning is as much of a valuable learning tool as the play itself. The assignment that has developed from these class discussions asks students to write a narrative (i.e., tell a story) that captures a meaningful experience in their use of language, writing, or acquisition of literacy. In sharing this story, students aim to teach their readers something about language or literacy, how language functions, how language shapes one's identity, how it reflects one's cultural upbringing, and/or how this experience has affected them. The students' writing responses to *Los Vendidos* certainly explore the origins of current attitudes about diverse groups experiencing inequitable treatment in the country, while they also probe the rhetorical situations of language, literacy, and writing in relation to constructs of empowerment, identity, and culture within a vast range of socioeconomic frameworks. Subsequently, by writing about the cultural misconceptions and injustices that motivate *Chicanx* theater and the plot of the play, students have the opportunity to examine the toxic immigrant rhetoric through the lens of the individuals and groups being directly targeted by the Trump administration.

As mentioned in this collection's introduction, my course aims to synthesize a writing-to-learn approach with a writing-as-process assessment design and culminating in student projects that critically engage issues around immigration, the nation, and belonging. Teaching at a Title V institution with an over 60 percent Hispanic student population, many of my students can directly relate to the effects of social injustice that is inherent in the play's central message. Through reflection and in various styles of articulation, the class works toward a general conclusion that challenges preconceptions and gets to the root of the indignation many Mexicans and Chicana/o people feel. Although the play takes on a satirical, self-deprecating form, the subject matter is very serious and shows that people are not mere tools to be used by others for their own needs. By identifying Valdez's intentional use of satire, students are able to discuss the stereotypes in the play more freely, but most important, they are able to critically analyze what these stereotypes reveal about our culture at large and the discourses at play when considering ethnic and linguistic differences. While many of my students are from Mexican and Mexican-American backgrounds of varying legal status in the United States, the humorous tone of the play allows for them to probe more critically into very serious topics of immigration and deportation. Many students express concern about stereotyping a race or ethnicity, an issue compounded by our former president Donald Trump's derogatory remarks about Mexicans and immigrants. By identifying and describing the stereotypes that Valdez is satirizing, students are able to express through both formal written assignments and class discussion posts their concerns about such negative assertions and their destructive imprints on society, and whether or not they are the individuals being targeted.

If our job is to guide students to make effective rhetorical choices in both their writing and reading, then it is critical to introduce them to texts that not only inspire them to write well, but to help them question how these rhetorical choices can be impactful in their lives outside of the classroom. Our job as educators extends beyond the classroom into our communities, and what better way to help prepare our students to negotiate their futures than by incorporating multiple theoretical and methodological approaches in our pedagogies that includes transcultural perspectives? Our students are coming from various multiethnic, socioeconomic, and other diverse cultural backgrounds, so it seems natural for them to draw from these experiences to make well-informed rhetorical decisions. As geopolitical borders are more frequently shifting, we can help them prepare for these transformations by considering how previous generations reacted to major, and often disorienting, cultural shifts in the past.

In *Los Vendidos,* Valdez is addressing a range of borders including the literal geopolitical one between Mexico and the United States, the cultural borders that emerge there, the linguistic borders these individuals navigate, and the borders between what separates robots from humans. In Chicanx literature and cultural studies, discussion largely adheres to border conflicts. The United States–Mexico borderlands often mark the interstitial space of fluctuating identity between the individual, the community, and the dominant culture. Writing from a hybridized space, Chicanx writers demonstrate the changing and multiple dynamics that occur in the borderlands and thus create a subjective matrix of cultural politics. According to Arturo Aldama and Naomi Quiñonez, current Chicana/o cultural studies are engaged in extracting meaning from a cultural aesthetic that has long been omitted from Euro-Western cultural canons and seeks to chart how subaltern cultural production of the United States–Mexico borderlands speaks to local hemispheric, and globalized power relations (2). "How can I be without border?" This is a question that haunts the Chicana/o imagination, framed in discussions about cultural schizophrenia, language debates, ancestral legitimacy, interstitial spaces, and mestiza/o consciousness. Discursive production on the border includes the formation of nationalism, directionality, imagined homelands, and how multiple ethnic perspectives construe identity.

For Chicanas/os, the borderlands and the immigrant experience represent the interstitial space between two or more cultures, languages, and histories that is both a place of hope and of loss, and where authors can explore and subvert hegemonic ideologies that have shaped Chicanx identity all across the United States. The border, as many Chicanx scholars including Gloria Anzaldúa, Héctor Calderon, and José David Saldívar have pointed out, is a literal geopolitical military zone as well as a spatial conception of cultural and linguistic conflict; it is not just an objective locale, but also a metaphor for identity. Scholarship emphasizes the mutability of the borderlands and the difficulties of positively defining the limits of its space. These observations reveal the mutability of the border and of border culture, and help to shed light on the social, political, and economic relationships and tensions that Chicanas/os explore in their writing. By considering the cultural and political currency of ethnic literature as a possible integral part of a standard undergraduate education in the United States, my goal is to demonstrate how these stories, via *Los Vendidos,* can motivate constructive discourse about critical consciousness/*conscientizacíon*, and help us to explore the intersections between ethnic, Latinx, and hemispheric studies on a global scale in the context of rhetoric and writing studies.

WORKS CITED

Aldama, Arturo J., and Naomi H. Quiñonez, editors. *Decolonial Voices: Chicana and Chicano Cultural Studies in the 21st Century.* Indiana University Press, 2002.

Bagby, Beth. "El Teatro Campesino Interviews with Luis Valdez." *The Tulane Drama Review,* vol. 4, 1967, p. 70. EBSCOhost, doi:10.2307/1125139.

Bolt, Julie. "Teaching Los Actos of Luis Valdez." *The Radical Teacher,* vol. 91, 2011, p. 71.

Broyles-Gonzalez, Yolanda. *El Teatro Campesino: Theater in the Chicano Movement.* University of Texas Press, 1994.

Cizmar, Paula. "Luis Valdez." *Mother Jones,* Jun. 1979, p. 52.

García, Ofelia, and Li Wei. *Translanguaging: Language, Bilingualism and Education.* Palgrave Macmillan, 2014.

Heredia, Roberto R., and Jeffrey M. Brown. "Bilingual Memory." *The Handbook of Bilingualism,* edited by Tej K. Bhatia and William C. Ritchie, Blackwell, 2008, pp. 224–249.

Huerta, Jorge A. "El Teatro's Living Legacy: After 50 Years Luis Valdez's Company Retains Both Its Chicano Identity and Its Broader Mission. Next: The Return of the Troupe's Most Famous Creation, Zoot Suit." *American Theatre,* vol. 10, 2016, p. 28.

M.E.CH.A Movimiento Estudiantil Chicanx de Aztlán. 5 Nov. 2017. http://www.mechanationals.org/2017/.

Montez, Noe. "Latinx Theatre as We Know It in the U.S. Is Only Half a Century Old, but Its Roots Are Deep and Its Future Boundless." *American Theatre,* vol. 10, 2016, p. 22.

Navarrette, Ruben, Jr. "Vendido." *Hispanic,* vol. 2, 2007, p. 14.

The San Francisco Mime Troupe. *The San Francisco Mime Troupe,* 2005. https://www.sfmt.org/about-us.

Valdez, Luis. *Actos.* Arte Público, 1971.

Valdez, Luis. "Los Vendidos Actos." Arte Público, 1971.

Valdez, Luis. "The Shrunken Head of Pancho Villa." *Mummified Deer and Other Plays.* Arte Público, 2005.

Worthen, W. B. "Staging América: The Subject of History in Chicano/a Theater." *Theater Journal,* vol. 49, no. 2, May 1997, pp. 101–120.

6

NARRATIVES AND COUNTERNARRATIVES
Contextualizing Immigrant Voices

Tuli Chatterji

In his interview with John Schilb in *College English*, Samrat Upadhyay writes, "It's interesting to look at the writer as a translator, and it's especially interesting to consider what happens if we consider all writers, regardless of ethnic background, as translators of the human experience" (557). When we begin to view writing through the lens of translating, notions of exclusion, othering, and marginalization start to become unobscured. Writing becomes a vehicle for inscribing, challenging, determining, or even crossing identity boundaries. And as such, student writers who are products of both dominant and marginalized groups can provide special insights into the ways in which writing pedagogy can affect views of justice and equity in the immigrant experience. This essay will focus on how a global perspective in a first-year composition classroom helps immigrant students document their journeys and identify their experiences through which they strategically negotiate their identity while choosing to become American and/or not. Though the study of humanities, as Gayatri Spivak rightfully reminds us, is "worldly, not global," in this essay I use the term global to be in dialogue with the Global Learning core competencies of LaGuardia Community College of City University of New York, where I conducted my present research. LaGuardia Community College defines Global Learning as "a critical analysis of and an engagement with complex, interdependent global systems and legacies (such as natural, physical, social, cultural, economic, and political) and their implications for people's lives and the earth's sustainability."

The essay will argue for the importance of incorporating lived experiences of students into the curriculum to help them identify the relationship between power and politics and in turn encouraging them to destabilize the dichotomies that privilege one group over another.

https://doi.org/10.7330/9781646421664.c006

While a close examination of student voices will focus on how immigrant students, mostly from non–English-speaking countries, view justice and equity, I also aim to discuss how critical pedagogy facilitates and legitimizes narratives that have the potential to alter the misconceptions and assumptions that US-born students might have toward languages, cultures, and nations outside their familiar spaces. I echo Arjun Appadurai, who in his essay "Disjuncture and Difference" states that the new "global cultural economy has to be seen as a complex, overlapping, disjunctive order that cannot be understood in terms of existing center-periphery model" (468). Unarguably, while close reading of global literary texts allows students to witness "a complex, overlapping" of pluralistic narratives and ideologies, I argue that it also helps foster a conversation in which students experience and engage with opposing views instead of participating in mutual exoticization or in an act of admiration/pity/sympathy for the "Other." Locality and nationality enter into a dialogue initiating new understandings in the relationship between dominant ideologies and powerful silences.

AIM OF THE STUDY

It was during my third semester as an English faculty member at City University of New York's LaGuardia Community College that I started identifying a pattern of desire among immigrant students to assimilate with prevalent ideas of *being* American, to an extent where it did not seem unusual for some to distance themselves consciously from their own languages and cultures. In one of the reflective essays that followed a discussion on our unit of "Englishes and Unidirectional Monolingualism" (which I will be discussing later), Susan, a freshman, voiced her thoughts:

> It was the summer of 1993. I was six years old when we moved to America. . . . I come from a small town in Dominican Republic. My life had changed and this was just the start. . . . Once the summer ended and school began I was introduced to new cultures and languages . . . I remember in my third grade I gave a speech in English in front of the entire school. That day was the day I felt accepted.

The above excerpt contextualizes a memory of a separation from a familiar territory (Dominican Republic) and a desire to embrace "new cultures and languages" in America. What is significant is the urgency to be "accepted," and that Susan associates her ultimate feeling of being accepted with the first time she displayed her proficiency in English language to her peers. Nowhere in her essay does she mention her pride as a fluent Spanish speaker. Susan's hopeful tone ("this was just the start"), indicating that her migration from Dominican Republic to the United States would enable a promising future, reinforces the subtle ways in which a binary between nations and languages slowly affects students' choices, identities, and narratives in ways often leading them to feel ashamed of their national origin, race, or culture. Reading narratives such as Susan's encouraged me to reflect and revise my pedagogical practices with the following research questions in mind:

a. What potentialities can global learning foster in a classroom where histories, cultures, languages, accents, and nationalities meet? Can it facilitate a constructive repositioning of students as both subjects and objects in narratives of oppressor and oppressed?

b. Does a diverse classroom naturally endorse diversity?

c. How do immigrant students resist, perpetuate, and negotiate with popular representations of their community that does not always speak in favor of them?

METHODOLOGY

For my study, I did qualitative research of student essays over four semesters with a range of forty-five to fifty students per semester. While the holistic approach of the course stayed almost the same—I divided the syllabus into separate short units addressing language, race, culture, and gender—the assigned readings and the assignments changed with every semester. The purpose of the revision was to rethink a broader cohesive learning framework that would strengthen my pedagogy while also facilitating a movement from content instruction to content exploration. As the aim of the present research was to identify how deep learning strengthened student voices, I focused on: (a) classroom participation, (b) research essays, and (c) literacy narratives to identify *how* and *when* immigrant students expressed resistance against structures of power and in *what* ways they challenged the status quo to address inequity and injustice toward them, and if they were willing to engage in such conversations at all.

DEMOGRAPHY

City University of New York's LaGuardia Community College, with a population of 18,533 students, representing 158 countries and 98 different languages ("Institutional Profile" 1), serves as an incredible resource to explore multiple possibilities of a global pedagogy. LaGuardia takes pride both in its diverse student population and the opportunity it provides in educating its first-generation college students, who make up 50 percent of the student population. With 48 percent Hispanic, 23 percent Asian, 17 percent Black, and 12 percent White students, a LaGuardia classroom unequivocally becomes a site where cultures, races, languages, and nations meet and clash to produce new understandings of bodies, borders, and binaries.

I based my study on my class, which was comprised of students from China, Greece, Jamaica, Guyana, Africa, Pakistan, Nepal, Ecuador, El Salvador, Mexico, Puerto Rico, Bangladesh, India, Korea, and Dominican Republic. Only 11 percent of the students in the study refused to be identified as hyphenated Americans even after acknowledging that they were born to parents who have not yet learned the English language.

IDENTIFYING THE PROBLEM

On the first day of every semester of my English 101: An Introduction to Expository Writing course, I ask my students to write me a letter stating their expectations from the course. Invariably, their needs always veer toward assisting them in learning techniques of fixing grammar, knowing strategies of writing transition sentences, and writing introductions or conclusions, to name a few. While I agree on the importance of English as a tool for success in American academia, what strikes me most is the lack of confidence and a feeling of *deficiency* about their capabilities that weighs heavy in the minds of my students, mostly immigrants. A first-generation immigrant myself and an English department faculty member who received most of her education outside the United States, I'm highly conscious of the conflicts, dissonances, struggles, and the desires within my immigrant students to assimilate with mainstream American culture. I recognize, to echo Albert Memmi's analysis, the ambivalent relationship of the "colonized mentality"—of both contempt for and "passionate" attraction to the colonizer (Freire 45). I also do not want to undermine the significance of learning academic English nor want to ignore the benefits of knowing Standard English in the job market. But what concerns me more are the ways in which internalization of dominant ideologies shapes immigrant students' identity and compels them to sometimes perpetuate the same hierarchies that they had earlier resented. In order to disrupt the cycle of inequity, as instructors we need to be vigilant of these transformative moments and educate students of the consequences of such transformations. I therefore identify a need to address and, if possible, theorize immigrant student voices in conversation with transnational literary texts to show how a critical engagement with social issues can initiate a discussion on equity and justice and prevent the perpetuation of ideologies to which most immigrant students often feel victimized. In this essay, I focus on student conversations on race, culture, and language as visible signifiers of discrimination.

THEORETICAL FRAMEWORK: WHY GLOBAL?

LaGuardia's mission of "educat[ing] and graduat[ing] one of the most diverse student populations in the country to become critical thinkers and socially responsible citizens" echoes postcolonial philosophy's disengagement with colonial practices to envision justice and equality for all. Indisputably, designing a global pedagogical framework that would celebrate individual perspectives without being reductive in approach can become a challenge for many instructors, who themselves might not be aware of the histories and cultures of their immigrant students. However, this limitation of instructors can be beneficial, as it helps create a learning site where the students' role is brought to task, thereby reinforcing educational philosopher John Dewey's (1859–1952) prediction that we can only create a lasting effect on our education system when we start incorporating the experiences of our students in building our pedagogy (Vavrus 4).

I extend Binaya Subedi's use of the term "global" in his article "Decolonizing the Curriculum for Global Perspectives," in which, instead of suggesting a split between the local and global, he advocates a need for a dialogue between local(s) and global(s) that "are complexly interconnected within the axis of power and politics" (623). In this essay, I propose a global approach to student writing that would, in part, include an examination of students' transnational experiences and perceptions of ideological matrices between structures that oppress and those who are oppressed, narratives which then can be used to lead a discussion on individual roles in destabilizing systemic forms of oppression. For instance, in one of the units in my English 101 course, I have students share an oppressive experience that altered their beliefs of their immediate surroundings. Each student was expected to use his experience as a tool of inquiry to explore it in the context of other issues, focusing more on the causes of oppressive behavior than on the effects. In one such situation, a first-generation immigrant Tibetan student narrated her humiliating high school experience in a Hispanic-majority classroom. Her joy seeing brown-skinned students as she entered her new classroom—whom she mistakenly assumed to be Indians—soon turned into a nightmare after learning the extent to which her classmates could bully her for her accent and her ignorance of American culture. In front of her present classmates (many of whom were Hispanic in origin), she justified her anger against those former classmates, mentioning how the incident not only left a permanent emotional scar within her but also eventually made her transfer to another school. Unhesitatingly, she pointed out her then classmates' lack of national, geographical, and cultural knowledge of Tibet.

What was striking about the above narrative is the many ways it reminds us of the need to decentralize the curriculum to foster ethical engagement and global self-awareness within our students. First, what we see here is not a binary between white/colored, but a brown/brown foregrounding and reproducing systematic forms of colonial oppression seen historically between whites/people of color. Second, the Tibetan student's non-American accent (later leading to a discussion on English-only movements) acts as a signifier of her alien status, and in this specific context, allowed the otherwise colonized Hispanic students to emerge as the colonizers. The Hispanic students, as can be understood, might have experienced the same feeling as the Tibetan student and may have taken this opportunity to assume their superior status. Third, Hispanic students' lack of knowledge about Tibet also parallels the Tibetan student's ignorance (of which she is unconscious) of the presence of brown-skinned people other than Indians. By reductively associating all brown people as South Asians, the student participates in racial profiling based on incomplete knowledge. Fourth, and not the least, both the Hispanic students and the Tibetan student situate themselves within the matrix of a colonial discourse and fail to demonstrate any disengagement with colonial enterprises of controlling the "other."

Similar to the Tibetan student, Danna, a young Dominican, expresses her frustration while reflecting on trying to "fit in" as a newly arrived immigrant in an ESL classroom in her high school. Danna narrates how she soon became an object of fun and laughter both because of her accent and her nationality. Quick to point out that Dominicans are often judged as "loud and violent people," what was interesting in her narrative is her reference to hearing other Hispanic students say that as a "Dominican" she "ain't gonna be anyone in lives." It took her little time to start seeing herself from the perspective of her race, language, and nationality and to understand the complexity of her identity as a Hispanic in United States. However, in her reflective essay, Danna writes:

But mi madre siempre me decia, mi hija no te preocupes nadie es mejor
que nadie, todos somos iguales y deberias de siempre tartar lo mejor de ti
no importa si no es perfecto pero nadie lo es. Yo siempre tuve pendiente
lo que mi madre hoy en dia me sigue dicendo, esa pequena frase.

Her decision to include, in Spanish, her mother's voice in her essay asking her to be proud of who she is and to try her best alters the hierarchical relation between nations and languages that she has experienced
and which she chooses to resist.

One can argue that narratives like these, and some as we will see in
the context of "Cross-Cultural Conversations" and "Englishes and Uni-
drectional Monolingualism," are reflective of a deficit model where the
"mental universe" of immigrant students of color or culture are colonized to an extent where they see each other as "lacking 'better' values";
where the better becomes synonymous with West and white (Subedi
623). The relationship between words and worlds is deep and profound:
in striving to read and write *words*, students forge a deep connection with
the ways in which they perceive their *worlds*.

The challenges, however, of countering neocolonialism are specifically felt in classrooms where immigrant students come from nations
that benefited directly or indirectly—economically or culturally—from
Western aid/influence. Subedi draws our attention to the deficit
approach of our global curriculum that often invests in "reinforcing
colonial, white racial ideology" instead of encouraging voices of dissent or transnational experiences similar to or in contrast with the
West (623). This reinscription of white ideology results in college
graduates sometimes being unable to communicate across differences,
thus failing to create a more ethical society for themselves and others. The cultural deficiency model primarily reduces the world into
two categories: the progressive, empowering West *and* the inferior,
uncivilized cultures of the rest of the world. The limited recognition
of the cultural capital of minority student population contributes to
the perpetuation of the deficit scheme that, as Subedi notes, "conflates
Eurocentrism with universalism and approaches questions of humanity and culture [only] through Western epistemologies" (624). Vavrus
confirms Subedi by stating how an assumption that minority students
are "culturally disadvantaged [in their] histories, belief, and conduct"
prevents appropriation of what researchers Luis Moll and Norma
Gonzalez term as "funds-of-knowledge" (Vavrus 7). From a Freirean
perspective, such an approach prevents students from treating the
world as an object that they can shape and alter with their individual
and collective experiences: "Learners are to understand how [the

world] has been made into *what it is* by what (other) humans have done, and failed to do" (Lankshear 111).

Incorporating funds of knowledge will prevent continuing systems that support the deficit scheme, thereby leading students to be critical of the myth of the "United States as a beacon of freedom and equality" (Tanenbaum and Miller 46). It can also lead us to ask: How can faculty draw from insights into our students' cultures and backgrounds to create classroom activities and lesson plans that are both relevant to student lives and build skills necessary to help students do well in college? In their book *How Learning Works: 7 Research-Based Principles for Smart Teaching* (2010), Ambrose, Bridges, Lovett, DiPietro, and Norman throw light on the Hardiman-Jackson model of development of social identity by referring to eight stages that lead to a holistic development of students—naïveté, acceptance, resistance, immersion, disintegration, redefinition, and internalization. Global curriculum, I argue, allows a shift from a quantitative view of knowledge to a qualitative approach that takes into account the immigrant student's learning in his home country to situate that knowledge in conversation with and not in opposition to his learning in the present context. It also facilitates students to creatively engage with pluralistic perspectives of their own identity (how they view themselves in dialogue with how they are viewed by others) to reach the stages of redefinition and internalization that challenge the dominant-minority dichotomy. In my study, I noticed students mostly remaining locked in the acceptance stage in which they internalize stereotypes that have been assigned toward them and are also not always willing to question preconceived notions they might themselves have toward other communities.

One way to encourage students to probe into narratives of marginalization or stereotype formations is to have them assume the role of a translator of their experiences to reflect on the complex interconnectedness of nations and cultures both through assigned readings and their real-life experiences. Reflection, as Don J. Kraemer notes, is "a combination of personal thoughts and critical thinking in order to fully understand a concept and/or what you did well or didn't do well" (610). When students use their own narratives to transcribe and reflect social perceptions and cultural myths, they start to contextualize the "productive tension" (607) and see those moments as opportunities for self-examination. Culturally responsive teaching (CRT), as M. Vavrus notes, forges a "democratic, student-centered pedagogy" that incorporates and honors the cultural perspectives of the students and allows them to recognize the differences in which each community is stereotyped by the other. What emerges is identification of the limitations within a Eurocentric epistemological framework and a recognition of the deep-seated effects of European colonialism in an assumedly postcolonial context (Vavrus 11). It's important to note that such a shift does not suggest that students become representatives of the community they come from. Instead, from Freire's model of problem-posing method of education, students become critically conscious toward the world that has shaped them and in turn start identifying the problems at stake to confirm the relationship that "World and human beings do not exist apart from each other, they exist in constant interaction" (Freire 32).

STORIES AND COUNTER-STORIES

Circle of Memory

Legitimizing narratives on migration and displacement encourage students to contextualize and vocalize the tension of what Leela Gandhi describes as the "two stories" of a colonial scene: "the seductive narrative of power, and alongside that the counter-narrative of the colonized" (22). While the Tibetan student's experiences above compel us to notice the conflict between dominant ideologies and student desires to internalize them, Shamir, a twenty-year-old Bangladeshi student, had an altogether different approach to the conversation. In his essay on race, Shamir reflects on the popular stereotype and misinformation about the Bangladeshi community in United States, where they are often seen as taxi drivers:

> Yes, it is true, and I do agree that some Bangladeshis do drive Taxis for a living, but there are many who have other professions such as doctors, engineers, teachers, etc. . . . which hardly gets noticed.

Born in New York but raised in Bangladesh, Shamir does not consider himself an American even while his family identifies him as such. Fluent in English, he feels more at home in Jamaica or Hillside among his Bangladeshi friends and families and eloquently articulates his anger over the ways he is represented. He reacts to the rise in global intolerance toward undocumented immigrants, Muslim communities, and people of color by critically disrupting the "banking method of education" and initiating a "problem-posing" discussion that draws on the connection between his experiences of being marginalized as a Bangladeshi Muslim in America with how he was viewed in Malaysia (a predominantly Islamic nation) at the wake of the terrorist attack on Holey Artisan Bakery in Dhaka, Bangladesh on July 1, 2016. Shamir documents the harsh, disrespectful conditions in which Bangladeshi laborers are forced to live in Malaysia, where many migrate to escape the economic conditions of their country, echoing similar reasons for migration to the United States:

> Many of them are undocumented as well, but as social media and various news channels will say that they smuggled themselves or landed themselves illegally on Malaysian soil, the truth that many of them are lured there by Bangladeshi conmen who scam them and show them dreams of better job opportunities and a better life, will never present itself.

If we interpret Shamir's narrative in terms of John Dewey's theory of knowledge and valuation, we see Shamir first identifies the problem, then he locates and defines the problem. His inquiry into the problem leads him to understand that selective representation of his community often plays a major role in spreading misinformation about his community (Axtelle 47).

While Shamir voices his criticism of popular transnational representations of Bangladeshi Muslims, his writing becomes a vehicle to vent a painful memory:

> It was during the time of the terrorist attack that I also fell sick with fever and had to miss out on some of my classes. I received an email from the high school regarding my absences and was ordered to visit the coordinator's office. As soon as I visited the office, the coordinator started questioning me vigorously in a cold manner about my absences, "Where was I? What was I up to? Why I was missing out so much on classes? Am I affiliated with 'certain activities'?" Afterwards, she became more direct and started telling me that "the students who carried out the activities at the bakery incident, did not attend classes properly" and that "90% of Bangladeshis are the same." Indirectly, she assumed that I was affiliated with "terrorist activities." I was shocked, ashamed and felt like I was struck with a hammer. I wish I could talk back or protest, but I was in too much pain to say a single word.

Carlos Hernandez, a Puerto Rican immigrant from the Bronx echoes Shamir in many ways, reinforcing how one's race, neighborhood, class, and knowledge of English can act as significant signifiers of discrimination. Speaking of popular assumptions against the Puerto Rican community, Carlos writes:

> I believe it matters where you live because many people will judge you based on social class. Most times I sense people believe they're better than me when they view my building or block. My most recent encounter of misconception on how people view me occurred two weeks ago when I had to take my dog Blue to the veterinary hospital in Manhattan for a teeth cleaning. Initially everything was going well until it was time to speak to the doctor. I suspected I was being stereotyped because of the breed of

my dog (pit-bull) and my appearance. Many people assume pit-bulls are dangerous dog, and believe it even more when the owner is of the minority class. I began to feel uncomfortable when he started speaking about the finances as if I didn't have an idea of how costly the procedure would be or as if I wouldn't be able to afford it.

Both Shamir and Carlos draw our attention to dominant grids of representing immigrants: class, race, and religion. Both demonstrate Freire's problem-posing education to voice injustice and fight for emancipation. If Shamir's painful experiences stem from his religion, for Carlos it is his race, class, and nationality. As minorities, neither Shamir nor Carlos then had the courage to express their anger from being misinterpreted, which they now unhesitatingly recall and document in their research essay.

On the other hand, Zina, a hard-working, quiet-natured student who moved to New York from Egypt, admits to the many opportunities he has received in the United States that were quite difficult to imagine when he was in Egypt. While he reflects on freedoms he can exercise, such as sexual rights within the United States, he is also conscious of how others view him in the States. Similar to Shamir's experience in Malaysia and in New York, Zina writes:

I actually had to deal with stereotypes myself because people thought that all Egyptians are "terrorists," I would get called terrorist a lot in school and people made a lot of jokes about me carrying explosives. However, I just ignored them and it worked out well.

If both Shamir and Carlos overtly express dissent against social perceptions about their identity, Zina voicing his decision to ignore the comments of his peers suggests a strategic negotiation that he had to make on the grounds that returning to Egypt is no longer an option for him. Zina was aware that education would empower him and chose to ignore his peers to prove them wrong. Now, after four years since the incident, he reflects on the episode to remind us that, based on the circumstances, it was necessary for him to remain silent in order to challenge the stereotype against his nation and people. Each of the above students become subjects of a process through which they "overcome authoritarianism and an alienating intellectualism" (Freire 67) by critiquing the premises of their social construction.

The above excerpts, from research essays on the unit "Race: Deconstructing Narratives," emerged after an intensive discussion on Daniel Beverly Tatum's essay "Defining Racism: Can We Talk?" Short in-class assignments and group presentations on concepts such as systemic racism, prejudice, and white privilege encouraged students to understand the concepts in the contexts of history. Students were then asked to explore one or two issues from four different perspectives: (a) understanding how Tatum discusses the concept, (b) reflecting on the concept as experienced by the student, (c) close reading of any one secondary source—an article, documentary, NPR podcast, or movie from the perspective of the concept, and (d) analyzing how literary texts (readings such as Claudia Rankine's *Citizen,* Judith Cofer's "Volar," and those read in class) represent the concept.

The class as a whole worked on the above sections for a period of four weeks spanning four class hours per week. The main objective of the assignment was to assist students in demonstrating their understanding of Tatum's essay through analysis, reflection, application, and integration. Even though my students represented different cross sections of society aside from being first- or second-generation immigrants, being in class together did not guarantee a cross-cultural conversation. The embedded reflective component of the research essay facilitated students to draw connections between literary texts, theoretical apparatus, and their lives. Learning became personal as students engaged in "re-invention . . . restless . . . hopeful inquiry" to analyze their own lives in the context of the theoretical apparatus (Freire 53).

Once students drafted their research essay, I used the technique of "inkshedding" to initiate a dialogue among the students. First developed by writing teachers Russ Hunt and Jim Reither in the 1980s and discussed at length by James Lang in his book *On Course, inkshedding* (239) brought my immigrant and native-born students together to understand how each can contribute to the production of recreating knowledge. Each student while reading an essay of one of their peers gave detailed comments/questions on the right side of the essay's margin. Once they were done reading their peer's essay, they returned the paper to the author, who then answered the questions on the left side of the margin. This written dialogue continued for approximately twenty-five to thirty minutes, after which each student was asked to do a five-minute reflective freewriting on the paper they read. I followed the activity with an in-class discussion on the common themes addressed by all the papers and the ways in which they were addressed. We inferred that each essay used literacy narrative as the initial form through which inquiry and research were conducted. Important to note is that the assignment did not specify a topic. Instead, it encouraged students to *feel* their world, to tell their stories—which then gave them confidence to decide on a topic based on the position they took and the argument they developed with the readings and their own experiences. The process helped them identify patterns of oppression and realize the enormous value of counter-narratives to disrupt the cycle of violence. For instance, Ana, a student from El Salvador, writes: "Because I am Salvadorean, I am automatically categorized and stigmatized for being associated with an international criminal gang MS 13 and most importantly for being Hispanic." As she refers to Ava DuVernay's phenomenal documentary *13th* (released on Netflix in 2016), Ana mentions how, as a woman of color and being Hispanic, she believes that the 13th Amendment has in many ways failed the Black and Latina community. Reflective moments such as these free students from being silent receptors of information by transforming them into writers who write for what they care about instead of speaking on behalf of instructors.

Cross Cultural Conversation

To continue the above conversation on facilitating democracy and difficult dialogue in classrooms, I extended Binaya Subedi's call for decolonizing the curriculum through an assignment on a comparative analysis of two essays: Vietnamese-American writer K. Oanh Ha's short story "American Dream Boat" and Nepali writer Prajwal Ratna Vajracharya's literacy narrative "Ten Deities in a Suitcase." What motivated me to choose writings from Vietnam and Nepal was first, that except for my two Nepali students, not many were familiar with Nepal, and second, I wanted to disrupt the myth of a homogeneous Asian culture in the mind of many of my US-born students.

In her essay "American Dream Boat," K. Oanh Ha recalls her experiences as a six-year-old refugee escaping from the communist rule in Vietnam with her family to settle in Orange County, California in the 1980s. Reflecting on her marriage to a white man, Scott, the narrator addresses issues such as inter-cultural tensions, her desperate desire as a teenager to be a "full-fledged American" (69), her conscious attempt to erase her Vietnamese traditions, her accent, and her decision later to return to Vietnam to learn about her roots. Prajwal Ratna Vajracharya, on the other hand, a United States ambassador from Nepal on Sanskrit ways of healing, voices his scathing criticism about the materialistic life in New York City that fails to inscribe harmony, lasting friendship, peace, and compassion among people. To help students learn about the real-life stories of struggles and experiences of immigrants, I encouraged them to read the interviews in Warren Lehrer and Judith Salon's phenomenal book *Crossing the Blvd.* All the narratives spoke of the indomitable courage, determination, and eagerness of immigrants to carve an identity in a land far from their own. The scaffolded in-class assignments

aimed to assist students in identifying how literary representations confirmed or challenged their own understandings of "being American." It
was interesting to notice the range of interpretations that emerged from
their essays:

Cici (first-generation immigrant from China). I really understand why
Ha wants to become an American, and escapes her traditional culture. It's important to know that none of her friends has accents.
I can imagine that if she had accents, she would look like strange.
Therefore, when her parents try to keep instilling their culture on
her, she just wants to escape from her family. . . . Many people think
that the U.S. is the "Melting pot" because people have different cultures to live together but it is not . . . cultural barriers is the big problem in many immigrant families. . . . We need to accept the diversity
of cultures.

Ahmed (first-generation immigrant from Bangladesh). Prajwal does not
have a good job and health care. Thus, he worked around 16 hours
a day. . . . It is difficult to find a comfortable life in any new place
outside from his own community. As a personal experience, I have
been living in the United States for 2 years. When I came here first I
have the same language problem just like Prajwal had. . . . I remember when I looked for a job everybody asked that do I know Spanish
or not. I also heard from some people that I no speak English. Any
way later on, I had a job and now I am studying in school, learning
English, living with friends who are also Bangladeshi. So, now everything goes well just like Prajwal. Again, all of my above discussions
mean that It is hardly possible for anybody to live comfortably in outside of the person's own community.

Imran (first-generation immigrant from Pakistan). Prajwal mentions that
when he came to New York for the second time, he did not have a
translator; therefore, he stayed in the room because of the language
barrier. This can be very frustrating if you are new to the country and
your communication medium is different from natives. . . . Overall,
my life is very much similar to Prajwal's life in New York. I live in
Queens New York, and I am a first-generation immigrant, so I have to
work twice as hard just to make ends meet. This story gave me a lot to
think about and my life in New York.

Rey (second-generation immigrant from Puerto Rico). In Nepal, Prajwal
says that everyone is happy because people don't chase for the things
people in New York seek, instead Nepalians chase happiness and
nirvana. But of course, Nepal is not New York and New York is not
Nepal, respectively. . . . In New York people chase superficial things
like money and work and never have time for family and friends. But I
believe that is not too bad because New Yorkers hustle to put food on
the table for their families and at the end of the day, knowing you've
worked hard for a loving family is all you really need here. I don't
think New Yorkers have the privilege to relax like people in Nepal. . . .

> Prajwal could not handle the New York hustle and I believe I would
> not feel at home with Nepali culture. But life as an immigrant in New
> York is a harder hardship than being a New Yorker itself.
>
> **Noel (second-generation immigrant from Mexico).** Ha's trip to
> Vietnam helped her more to discover her roots. . . . She has been
> Americanized all these years that even though she grew up in a tra-
> ditional Vietnamese household, she was more Americanized and has
> forgotten her language in a sense. This reminds me of myself; last year
> when I went to Mexico, my Spanish was terrible and I "dressed" like
> an American forgotten my roots. Until I got there, my family always
> said your Mexican first not American, but I felt like that's not true
> because although I grew up in a somewhat traditional Mexican house-
> hold I always felt more American and I loved it.

The above excerpts from both first- and second-generation immigrant
students that emerged from their readings of two different forms of immigrant narratives compel us to think of the differences in voice, style,
and attitude toward "being American." While Cici, a recent migrant,
feels connected to Oanh Ha to conclude that an immigrant's accent can
act as an impediment to assimilation, Noel, a second-generation immigrant, does not share the same concern as Cici. Interestingly, Noel identifies himself as an American and overtly expresses his dissent against
being seen as a Mexican. Noel's denial of a hyphenated identity is a reminder of how students can internalize dominant oppressive narratives
against certain nations to an extent where they refuse to be identified
as an immigrant from that nation. While Noel echoes Memmi's analysis
of the colonized's attraction for the colonizer, and Freire's observation
that "self-depreciation is another characteristic of the oppressed" (45),
his narrative essentializes a binary that the study of humanities aims to
dismantle. On the other hand, like the narrator of "Ten Deities," both
Ahmed (Bangladeshi) and Imran (Pakistani) reinstate the difficulties of
living outside one's community and the challenges that accompany being a first-generation immigrant. In contrast, Rey, a New Yorker, shares
a voice similar to Noel but acknowledges that life can be way more challenging for an immigrant in New York than that of a New Yorker. What
is interesting about Rey's narrative is not only his conscious construction
of a hierarchy between the two nations but also his embedded assumption that he won't feel at home with Nepali culture even having never
visited Nepal. These narratives foreground the need to de-centralize a
Eurocentric curriculum so that students feel encouraged to be respect-
fully receptive toward other nations, cultures, and languages instead of
viewing the United States as the *only* standard or possible center that all
immigrant students should aspire for.

Englishes and Unidirectional Monolingualism:
Conversations on immigrants' desire to assimilate and adapt invariably led to the challenges that many of my students experienced while struggling to learn American Standard English and its accent. I took this opportunity to shift the focus to the history of British colonization and World Englishes. In a classroom where immigrant students start with the premise that their success in America depends on the extent to which they can assimilate with American norms, accents, and traditions, I had students read three essays: (a) nineteenth-century British imperialist Thomas Babington Macaulay's "Minute on Indian Education" in dialogue with (b) African novelist Ngugi wa Thiong'o's essay "Decolonizing the Mind" and (c) American writer Jake Jamieson's essay "The English-Only Movement: Can America Proscribe Language with a Clear Conscience?" The purpose of this approach was to decenter the power of American English and initiate a conversation on critiquing unidirectional monolingualism of America. If Macaulay's essay allowed students to notice *why* and *how* the English language spread in the colonies, reading Thiong'o helped students understand how colonization dominated the "mental universe of the colonized" to an extent where the colonized started to perceive himself through the culture of the colonizer. Contemporary writer Jamieson focuses on the debate of whether English should be the official language in America, therefore highlighting the linguistic perpetuation of colonial discourse: "Should immigrants be pushed toward learning English or encouraged to retain their native tongues?" Following the same strategy as Macaulay, Jamieson refers to how American politicians and legislators perpetuate the *supposed* superiority of American English over the native tongues, thereby compelling immigrant students to view their own knowledge of English as improper and incorrect. Jamieson's thought-provoking questions at the end of his essay acted as perfect starting points for the class to reflect on their own relationship with their everyday languages:

> Do we plan to allow everyone in this country the freedom of speech that we profess to cherish, or will we decide to reserve it only for those who speak the same language as we do? Will we hold firm to our belief that everyone is deserving of life, liberty, and the pursuit of happiness in this country? Or will we show the world that we believe in these things only when they pertain to ourselves and people like us? (Rosa and Eschholz 265)

Student Responses Were Equally Diverse
Alia (40-year-old mother): I should know I myself come from two parents that migrated to the United States, and yes I know I should have some

> consideration for the Spanish speaking community, Because mom is from Puerto Rico and speaks Spanish. . . . She has never learned to speak english well she speaks broken english and still does till this day it's been 50 yrs Plus since she came to the United States and you would think her english would be perfect by now. My husband is another great example when he came to the United states and met me he did not speak any english. But that all changed once he met me. I told him when we got married and moved in together, I said no one in my home speaks Spanish we all communicate in english. Spanish tv, music not happening, you see this is my second marriage and I have two sons from my first marriage and we only spoke to each other in english. So my husband had no choice but to learn the english language.

As can be seen from the above excerpt, Alia's visible struggle with the English language compels her to reinforce the English-only movement as the only way of becoming American. Alia relates with Amy Tan's "Mother Tongue" (which she read prior to writing her essay) and like Tan, is ashamed of her mother's "broken English," which, as she admits, she couldn't change. However, her policing of her husband, leaving him with no other choice than to learn English symbolizes the subtle ways in which immigrants' awareness of language hierarchy in America perpetuate linguistic colonization. One might assume that the student's previous experiences of being perceived as "deficient" also compelled her to essentialize the "assumed" hierarchy between English and Spanish in America.

Andry, a nineteen-year-old second-generation immigrant, echoes Alia's argument:

> To not speak English in America where English is the literal language is almost redundant to think of, just because America is a land of immigrants doesn't mean our government should conform to foreign languages. There still has to be defining aspects of America, we can't just become discombobulated. The claim that those pushing for an English only America is an attempt to discriminate is pretty headache inducing as there's no inequalities being applied to anyone and the only goal is to get everyone to speak English, rather than having someone losing ability to function or participate in American life because they can't speak English.

Disturbing and problematic as it may sound, Andry and Alia's resistance toward their native language complicates their approach to see English like any other language. Both have experienced, to use the words of Deepika Bahri, "the rocky terrain of otherness" (Lunsford 69) and are aware of the power and prestige of American English. Though both use their writing to express their voice, the sort of voice is concerning and problematic.

I agree that improvement in English writing skills is one of the keys to success in American academia, but as the focus of my concern is more on how a global curriculum can help students critique ethnocentrism or perpetuation of racial/cultural/linguistic borders, what we see here is the presence of challenges in attaining that goal. Nelson reminds us that "When approaching a *language* transplanted to a new cultural and linguistic context . . . one is brought to various realizations about the notion of language and the *varieties* that a language may develop" (327). He argues that the "cultural contexts that defined 'appropriateness' in the parent situation are not necessarily the same in the new situation" (327). Both of the students above chose to ignore the variations and the multilingual realities in the classroom, thereby reinforcing my previous argument that what students are missing is that languages are not simply tools for communicating; languages map rich cultural differences in ways of thinking, lived experiences, embodiment, and material life. So, it's not so much that students need to value other languages simply to make people feel good and included; it's more that by erasing those languages, they are erasing history, culture, and valuable ways of thinking that are contained within that language. By failing to acknowledge that even English has its own limitations when used as a tool to translate another culture or tongue, both Andry and Alia become silent participants of epistemic violence that continue to identify immigrant students as deficient learners.

Brianna Morales, an American-born Puerto Rican student, had an alternative viewpoint on language than Alia and Andry. Brianna is fluent in both English and Spanish and can easily pass as white. In her literacy narrative, she reflects on her visit to Puerto Rico where, as a child, she was bullied for being too "American." In her critical engagement of Vietnamese author Oanh Ha's short story "American Dream Boat," she departs from her desire to assimilate with whiteness and instead documents how the trip to Puerto Rico made her realize the importance of Spanish in her life. Unlike Noel, who wanted to be identified only as American while visiting his family in Mexico, Brianna is critical of how linguistic hierarchy between English and Spanish in America fails to do justice to the culture and traditions of Spanish-speaking immigrants:

> For many years there has been a repetition that immigrants who come to the US or people that have a different culture change themselves to adapt to the American culture. To become a part of the culture they often do three things: First, they hear stereotypes that they don't want to be a part of. Then, they realize they are different which makes them begin to feel abnormal, almost alienated. After that they take action and try to

change themselves. Both Liu and I looked down at ourselves because of the popular stereotypes attached to being Chinese or Puerto Rican. Like Chinese-American writer Eric Liu, Vietnamese-American Author Oanh ha, I too realize that we shouldn't change ourselves to fit in. Instead we should embrace the fact that we are all different in our own ways.

Brianna's critical self-introspection, her comparing of herself with Eric Liu's experiences, and her engaging in de-centering popular perspectives toward immigrants shift the focus from how the immigrant subject is viewed by others to how the subject can interpret him/herself.

Kyra, a twenty-four-year-old Ecuadorian student, similar to Brianna, unsettles the center-periphery model mentioned earlier, making discussion on World Englishes necessary to thwart authoritative discourses of power:

My mom's family are Ecuadorian, while my father's side are originally from Sweden and he was born in the United States. Naturally, I grew up with both of the language of my parents. But English was always a language that "gringos" spoke, a language that made me feel different from the rest. . . . I always felt uncomfortable speaking it. Nevertheless, English was part of my identity, although I still couldn't relate it to my culture. Two years ago, I was forced to embrace English as one of my languages. I moved to France and since I didn't fully speak French, I had to rely on English to communicate. When I did try to speak French, because of my strong accent, people would automatically switch to a half French, half English means of communication. At that moment, I saw language not only as a part of my identity but also as an important tool to participate in society and to see myself in the world surrounding me. Now that I live in New York City, English has once again transformed, and become the language I use at work and with most of my friends, still though, in my home, with my community, my sister and my roommate, we speak in Spanish. Speaking Spanish makes me feel at home and allows me to be fully myself. Spanish is my mother tongue so it carries and reflects "most" if not all of my identity. I live between two languages that theoretically uphold part of my identity, even though I argue that it is Spanish that best speaks my culture.

Kyra moves between languages without privileging one over the other. Through a close reading of Kenyan novelist Ngugi Wa Thiong'o's essay "Decolonizing the Mind," Kyra identifies how her experiences were similar to Thiong'o, who also felt English alienated him from his own culture. Reading selections of vernacular literature such as Jamaican dub poet Mutabaruka's "Dis Poem" (Ahmad) encouraged Kyra to demand a change in perspectives toward immigrants' use of the English language:

Should immigrants let go of their past culture and embrace American values to ease tensions that might arise when two or three different cultures meet? Language carries our identity; therefore, it can be used as a tool to dominate human beings. English has always found its way in through violence and discrimination to assume a superiority over other languages. When we say that English is a measure of intelligence and we allow people to think that other languages and tongues are poor and unintelligent we are shattering identities and reinforcing the thought that the colonizers were better than us.

She expresses her concern that ignoring the sociolinguistic reality of immigrants (or, in a pedagogical scenario, immigrant students) would not only be immoral and unethical but would also curtail the cognitive development of students who often have to struggle with the idea that their cultural and discursive differences are interpreted as deficient in academia.

Michael, another twenty-year-old first-generation immigrant (though from Greece, unlike Susan, from the Dominican Republic), extends Kyra's approach in consciously rejecting unidirectional monolingualism:

When I first stepped foot in this country, I could only speak Greek. My English vocabulary was limited to words like hi, good, thank you, etc. When I entered high school, I realized that English is the only way to move forward. As the years passed, I neglected Greek, and my proficiency in English increased. I was extremely proud until one day I realized the damage of this transformation when I could not translate a letter written for my mother in English to Greek. I could see a disappointment in her face: Her Greek raised boy was not able to translate English words to his native language. I would start speaking in Greek and, when I encountered a word which I did not know the meaning of, I would switch to English. Same thinking was applied when writing Greek.

Calling it "Greeklish," Michael saw it as a "problem" that he needed to correct. So, he decided to take some courses in Greek, which, as he wrote, "increased the fluency to a normal level," and he no longer had any difficulty in communicating with his parents without having to switch to English. Michael's analysis highlights situations where immigrant students tend to become monolingual English speakers. Narratives such as these establish the pedagogical importance of considering the strategic negotiations immigrant students make to construct their identities outside their country of origin.

Each of the above narratives contextualizes student reflection that in some way echoes Asao B. Inoue's questions that he raises in his book *Antiracist Writing Assessment Ecologies* (2015): "What are our students doing when asked to reflect?" (131). Each story enters into a dialogue with the other to attempt "to articulate and figure out *how* to handle uneven power relations that stem from . . . race [and] language practices" (141, italics mine). The excerpts also serve as active reminders of the need to be receptive toward immigrant students' previous knowledge as well as teaching methodologies that they were accustomed to before moving to United States. For example, Liu, a recent migrant from China articulated the misconceptions of which he has often been a victim:

> Good grades all come from efforts, not where people come from. During class time, many people have noticed that most of Chinese students are really quiet. Some people may say they are shy because they are not confident about talking in English. I do not totally agree with that. I think that it is because of cultural difference. The Chinese education system only promotes learning through rote learning and listening to the teachers' lecture, as opposed to the US method which encourages dialogue and independent learning. Besides, the average class size is above 45 in China so students are required to be quiet during class time since kindergarten. Otherwise, teachers will not be able to finish their lecture in 45 minutes. Over time, being quiet in class becomes a habit for us.

Liu draws our attention to how instructors' ignorance of immigrant students' culture and history can have a debilitating effect in learning where instructors can unwittingly play the role of a benevolent colonizer, assuming the role as subjects while relegating students as objects in the learning process.

CONCLUSION

The above study supports James Bank's content integration theory that offers students a tool to start exploring a topic from a pluralistic perspective: locally, nationally, and globally. While global awareness through a study of multicultural texts is crucial to facilitate a discussion on justice and equity, it is equally important to encourage students to draw connections with their previous knowledge and experiences and to use that as a platform to build knowledge. As instructors, it is not *what* we teach but *how* we teach that matters.

I agree that in a twelve-week semester the challenges are immense both for students and instructors, especially in courses such as First-Year Writing and Composition. Even then, I saw that when I divided my syllabus into theme-based small units and selected readings from the countries of my students, it helped prevent both US-born and immigrant students from exoticizing each other and instead helped them identify oppressive global structures of which they have been both victims and perpetrators.

Writing, as Angelika Bammer notes, "whether scholarly or creative, [is] a form of action. It [has] effects in the world" (130). Within a few weeks of the start of the semester, I realized that a diverse classroom does not necessarily guarantee diversity. Students like Andry, Noel, and Rey, in spite of being around classmates from China, Ecuador, Pakistan, and Jamaica, still held on to some of their prejudices about those nations and their peers. On the other hand, I also noticed that encouraging students to come up with their own topics for research papers instead of assigning them had its benefits; it increased their analytical, interpretive, and critical thinking skills to develop a personal relationship with their writing. Writing became a form of activism. Furthermore, "inkshedding" gave students not only an opportunity to reflect on the feedback and self-critique some of their previous assumptions; it also compelled them to engage themselves in a cross-cultural dialogue in which they had to interrogate their relationship with their own culture, language, and nationality.

Finally, designing a syllabus with a wide range of perspectives helped me to identify a range of student voices that either critiqued, perpetuated, or strategically negotiated with dominant discourses to define identity. Each of the students—Shamir (Bangladesh), Noel (Mexico), Kyra (Ecuador), Brianna (Puerto Rico), and others—responded from a position that was on either side of the dominant/subordinate binary. While Shamir critiqued the binary, Noel reinstated it, whereas Kyra and Brianna reflected on the consequences of perpetuating the dichotomy. Selecting non-Western writers who write from the West and yet draw perspectives of their native culture facilitated a discussion among students who felt empowered to see similar experiences documented and in print. At a time when the political atmosphere has proven difficult for our immigrant students to celebrate their nationality and culture, it is crucial that as educators we reinforce cultural sensitivity supporting Duffy's claim that in "critical pedagogy the highest value . . . is *justice*, the commitment to address and ultimately challenge the cultural practices and institutions that have produced oppression" (in Kraemer 622). Education will no longer suffer from "narration sickness" (Freire) once educators affirm immigrant students' narratives as invaluable resources for initiating critical and liberating dialogues of social change.

WORKS CITED

Ambrose, Susan A., Michael Bridges, Marsha C. Lovett, Mucele DiPietro, and Marie K. Norman. *How Learning Works: 7 Research-Based Principles for Smart Teaching.* Jossey-Bass, 2010.

Appadurai, Arjun. "Disjunction and Difference." *The Post-Colonial Studies Reader,* edited by Bill Ashcroft et al., Routledge, 2007, pp. 468–472.

Axtelle, George E. "John Dewey and the Genius of American Civilization." *John Dewey and the World View*, edited by Douglas E. Lawson and Arthur E. Lean, Southern Illinois UP, 1964, pp. 35–63.

Bammer, Angelika. "Introduction to 'How we Write Now.'" *PMLA*, vol. 133, no. 1, 2018, pp. 124–131.

Freire, Paulo. *Pedagogy of the Oppressed*. Continuum, 2000.

Gandhi, Leela. *Postcolonial Theory*. Columbia University Press, 1998.

Inoue, Asao B. *Antiracist Writing Assessment Ecologies*. Parlor Press, 2015.

Kraemer, Don J. "The Good, the Right, and the Decent: Ethical Dispositions, the Moral Viewpoint, and Just Pedagogy." *College Composition and Communication*, vol. 68, no. 4, 2017, pp. 603–628.

LaGuardia Community College. "Institutional Profile." 2020, https://www.laguardia.edu/uploadedfiles/main_site/content/ir/docs/institutional-profile-2020.pdf.

LaGuardia Community College. "Outcomes Assessment and Definitions of LaGuardia Community College, CUNY, Core Competencies." https://www.laguardia.edu/Assessment/Resources/.

Lang, James J. *On Course*. Harvard UP, 2008.

Lankshear, Colin. "Functional Literacy from A Freirean Point of View." *Paulo Freire: A Critical Encounter*, edited by Peter McLaren and Peter Leonard, Routledge, 1995, pp. 90–118.

Lehrer, Warren, and Judith Salon. *Crossing the Blvd*. W. W. Norton & Company, 2003.

Lunsford, Andrea A., and Lahoucine Ouzgane, editors. *Crossing Borderlands: Composition and Postcolonial Studies*. University of Pittsburg Press, 2004.

Macaulay, Thomas Babington. "Minute on Indian Education." *History of English Studies*, 2 February 1835, Web. http://oldsite.english.ucsb.edu/faculty/rraley/research/english/macaulay.html.

Mutabaruka. "Dis Poem." *Rotten English*, edited by Dohra Ahmad, W. W. Norton & Company, 2007, pp. 85–89.

Nelson, Cecil L. "My Language, Your Culture: Whose Communicative Competence?" *The Other Tongue: English Across Cultures*, edited by Braj B. Kachru, U of Illinois Press, 1992, pp. 327–339.

Oanh Ha, K. "American Dream Boat." *One World, Many Cultures*, 8th ed. edited by Stuart Hirschberg and Terry Hirschberg, Pearson, 2012, pp. 68–72.

Rosa, Alfred, and Paul Eschholz, editors. *Models for Writers*. Bedford/St. Martin's, 2012, pp. 261–268.

Spivak, Gayatri Chakravorty. "How Do We Write, Now?" *PMLA*, vol. 133, no. 1, 2018, pp.166–170.

Subedi, Binaya. "Decolonizing the Curriculum for Global Perspectives." *Educational Theory*, vol. 63, no. 6, 2013, pp. 621–636.

Tanenbaum, Laura, and Karen Miller. "Internationalizing 'America': Critical Pedagogy in the Multinational Community College Classroom." *International Journal of Critical Pedagogy*, vol. 5, no. 2, 2014, pp. 37–53.

Thiong'o, Ngugi wa. "Decolonising the Mind." *Decolonising the Mind: the Politics of Language in African Literature*, 1 February 2018, https://ngugiwathiongo.com/decolonising-the-mind/.

Upadhyay, Samrat, and John Schilb. "Writing Cross-Culturally." *College English*, vol. 74, no. 6, 2012, pp. 554–566.

Vavrus, Michael. "Culturally Responsive Teaching." *21st Century Education: A Reference Handbook*, edited by Thomas L. Good, Sage, 2008, pp. 519–527.

7

CLASSROOMS FILLED WITH STORIES
Writing Immigrant Narratives in the Age of Trump

Libby Garland and Emily Schnee

IMMIGRANT STORIES AT BROOKLYN'S COMMUNITY COLLEGE

When we walk into our classrooms, we walk into spaces filled with stories of migration. There is Hugo, whose recently deported mother has just made her way back from Mexico to her family in Brooklyn, arriving with an ankle injury sustained on the dangerous journey across the border. There's Safiya, whose mom fled Egypt in the wake of a rancorous divorce, overstayed her tourist visa, and spent six long, pivotal years without seeing her adolescent daughters. There's Alicia from Guyana, who still misses the mango tree that grew in the yard of her family home. There's Mohammed, who was born in the United States but raised in Pakistan after his undocumented parents fled New York in the anti-Muslim aftermath of 9/11. There is Habib, whose mother hates his father's practice of hosting any newly-arrived fellow Bengali who needs a place to stay—a waste of precious household resources, she says. And there's Azeez from Nigeria, who dresses like a British schoolboy and fervently reaffirms his belief in the American dream in every essay.

These are our students at Kingsborough Community College, the City University of New York's two-year college in Brooklyn where we teach history and English, respectively. In this chapter, we examine the meanings of reading and writing immigrant stories in Libby's US immigration history and Emily's composition classes, particularly in the era of President Donald Trump. Over forty percent of our students were born abroad and many more are the children of immigrants ("National Origins"). Thus, immigrant stories have immediate personal, pedagogical, and political salience in our classrooms. In what follows, we explore the ways our students narrate and interpret immigrant stories. We intentionally echo the forms of analysis we ask from our students: we hew closely to the stories of our classrooms, and then place those stories in our larger institutional and political context.

https://doi.org/10.7330/9781646421664.c007

We have spent years reading and reflecting upon our students' explorations of immigrant stories, and, in turn, developing our curricula and writing assignments to foster those explorations. Each of us has experimented over the years with how to get students to put their personal stories of migration—or the stories of people they know and love—in conversation with the larger historical and literary narratives we study. As it happens, we have landed on pedagogies that approach this project from precisely opposite directions. Emily begins each semester of her composition classes by asking students to engage deeply with the personal. As part of her classes' semester-long exploration of immigration, the first drafted essay assignment is to write a profile of an immigrant to the United States. Given the students' backgrounds, the vast majority of them choose to interview a family member or close friend. Emily aims for this deceptively simple narrative assignment to lead students into critical inquiry into the dominant discourse around immigration, even as students struggle to situate the experience of one individual within the political, economic, and social trends that motivated their migration and shaped their experiences of the United States. In starting with the personal, Emily follows in the footsteps of a long, albeit contested, tradition of composition scholars and practitioners who have sought to bring personal writing to the center of our classrooms (Bloom; Elbow; Fontaine and Hunter; Kimball et al.; Spigelman, "Argument and Evidence," "Personally Speaking"). In so doing, Emily hopes that the students will, through their essays, collectively produce a foundational course text, one that allows peer review to become not just an exercise in developing one's writing skills, but an opportunity for students to critically explore the intersections, and discrepancies, in the experiences of immigrants from countries as diverse as Uzbekistan and Cameroon.

As the semester progresses in Emily's course, the class moves from texts produced by students to reading published texts which, in turn, lead the group into a final research essay. In that project, students must integrate information from at least one source they have read during the semester with independent research to write a position paper on some aspect of immigration. Though Emily designed the essays as a progression in terms of their increasing complexity as writing assignments—from narrative to text-based analysis to research essay—she sees that they also represent a progression in terms of students' ability to apply a more critical lens to the immigrant story.

Meanwhile, Libby's class, which explores the history of immigration to the United States, starts with the big picture rather than with personal narratives. Her class spends most of the semester exploring historical scholarship reflecting a range of approaches to the subject. The class reads about the evolution of US immigration law and policy, including histories of the implementation of Chinese Exclusion, the rise of border control, the growth of an immigrant detention and deportation regime, the institution of "guest workers," and questions about asylum seekers and immigration bans. Students also study social and cultural dimensions of immigration, such as how newcomers' lives, and those of their families, have been shaped by the spaces they have moved through in towns and cities across the country: workplaces, streets, housing, schools, courts, movie theaters, churches. Throughout, the class explores how individual stories do and don't reflect larger narratives—of success, of "Americanness," of "foreignness," or of "legality." It is only in the last third of the semester or so that Libby asks students to think through their own relationship to history by identifying what they find to be the most compelling theme that has emerged from our reading, and then developing a question around that theme to write about. If students choose, they can address that question using their own experience or that of their family, as well as drawing on the material from the course. Many, given their immigrant backgrounds, opt to do this. Some of those who write about their own stories even opt to post them publicly on a website Libby's students created some years back, specifically to document and showcase how Kingsborough students' own experiences are part of the larger fabric of US immigration history. Like Emily's class, then, Libby's often calls on students to engage with scholarly questions via personal narratives, and vice versa.

While we move in opposite directions in terms of conceptual scale—Emily from the micro to the macro, and Libby the other way around—both of us nevertheless hope for similar outcomes in our courses: that our students come to see themselves as authorities, able to weigh in as scholars, as writers, as historians, and to write meaningfully about immigrant experiences. Framing our classes around this work is time-consuming, and sometimes frustrating, for us and for our students. It will come as no surprise to anyone who teaches to hear that our students' writing does not always achieve the aims we lay out for them. But both of us have stuck with it because we see the telling and interpreting of immigrant stories as part of the social justice enterprise of teaching. By grounding our curricula in immigrant stories, we hope to convey to our students that these stories matter and should be told. And we hope that students come to see the ways that these narratives both reflect and teach us about the politics of, and the stakes in, such issues as borders, identities, law, labor, war, and migration.

We recognize that what we are asking our students to do in such writing is no simple matter. This is true not only because many of our students struggle with writing and reading, but because the task of putting individual stories in conversation with larger forces, so fundamental to what good scholarship does, is inherently fraught. We understand that our assignments present both ethical and intellectual dilemmas about storytelling, textual and historical interpretation, and argument. Indeed, as we have worked together on this essay, we have come to realize that we must grapple with similar challenges: picking apart complex tales whose natures resist easy categorization and using them to explore questions of our own posing, rather than presenting stories on their own terms, in their original form. Does it do violence to people's tales to remove them from their contexts and impose one's own understandings on them? Or does it honor them, by drawing attention to the larger stakes involved? Both, naturally, and this is the dilemma of all such scholarship. When we ask students to analyze personal tales by linking them to, and explaining them in light of, larger structures, or when we ourselves analyze our students' words, we try to balance the tensions of honoring those voices as they are with illuminating them by pointing to the bigger reasons why they matter.

MAKING SENSE OF STUDENTS' STORIES

We recognize the singularities and complexities of all of our students' stories at the same time that we find notably similar threads when we look across our students' writing. Despite our different pedagogical starting places, disciplinary backgrounds, and course objectives, we both find that it is often challenging for our students to make the analytical leaps we coax them toward through assignments that ask them to connect the personal and individual, on the one hand, with larger social and historical forces, on the other. In looking closely at our students' writing across both our courses we find several common patterns that we wish to highlight in this chapter. First, there are those essays in which students draw pat conclusions about the nature of the immigrant experience, echoing dominant narratives about hard work, meritocracy, and the American Dream. Second, we encounter many essays that evoke the complex dynamics at play in a particular immigrant's life but retreat without fully analyzing these dynamics. Third, we sometimes do find essays that speak back boldly to pervasive myths and comment on the complexities inherent in the stories they tell. Finally, we have discovered that some students, by the end of the semester, are indeed able to reflect in sophisticated ways on the larger historical and political contexts of immigration, putting individual stories in conversation with the texts we have studied throughout the semester. In Libby's class, this means that some students are able to pose questions that lead them to examine the continuities and disconnects between personal narratives and the longer arc of history. In Emily's class, students also seem most able to craft thoughtful analyses when they are writing in response to questions of their own posing, using the course texts, independent research, and the personal tales told at the beginning of the semester to advance an argument about immigration. In both of our classes, however, we have the sense that students who reach this more complex level of analysis do so precisely because personal stories have been welcomed into our classrooms.

Pattern #1: Pat Conclusions

Despite our pedagogical ambitions, both of us remain struck by how difficult it is, even in the current polarized political context, to move many students away from magical thinking about the immigrant experience, or about the nation's myths about itself as the land of opportunity for all. The tropes of rags to riches, pulling oneself up by one's bootstraps, and achieving the American dream exert a powerful force on our students' imaginations despite, or perhaps even because of, so much evidence in their lives to the contrary. For many of them, too, a long history of essay-writing training geared largely to dashing off formulaic pieces of writing for standardized tests has left them with the conviction that their writing should begin and end with vague, grand pronouncements that gesture at taking a stand but, in reality, are fairly empty of insight. Our assignments are explicitly designed to counter this training, and we both push our students throughout their writing process to go beyond the obvious and cliché. Nevertheless, the end results often fall short of what we might wish.

Yuliya, a bright, hardworking, former actor from Belarus, typifies this pattern. She chose to write her immigrant profile about her aunt Daria, who left economic and political crises in their country to try her luck in the United States. Though Daria struggles with learning English and finding gainful employment after overstaying her tourist visa, she ends up meeting "a tall, handsome American" and "from that moment, [her] life changed in a way that she could not even imagine." Now, married with US citizenship, she has her own home and business, a US-born son, and recently went on vacation to China. Yuliya's narrative eschews any effort to analyze the structural factors that may have resulted in such a happy outcome and, instead, uses her essay to confirm her aunt's "belie[f] in destiny" that "turned [her life] into a real fairy tale." Yuliya concludes her narrative with the somewhat empty affirmation that "despite the fact that immigration, usually, is a long, hard process of adaptation, America is the best place in the world when [a] person can realize any dreams, possibility and successful[ly] achieve goals, always says my aunt."

In great contrast to Yuliya's fairytale narrative, Cecilia's profile details her undocumented Ecuadoran coworker's perilous journey to the United States, her fear of dying in the desert with her two young daughters, the discrimination she has faced in this country because of her immigration status, and her heartbreak at not being able to return to Ecuador to see her ailing father. Yet, after four pages spent describing these hardships, Cecilia, too, falls back on clichés, concluding her essay with a baseless assertion that seems oddly disconnected to the story she has just told: "Jacqueline's story teaches us that life in the US can be a rollercoaster ride but if you stick to your plan everything should turn out fine." It is almost as if Cecilia cannot bring herself to acknowledge the lack of options her coworker faces given our current political climate for undocumented immigrants.

Other students had sympathetic but unsophisticated appraisals of immigrants based, at times, on the compassion or affection they feel for the person they profiled. These essays implicitly acknowledged the current anti-immigrant context but resorted to slogans rather than analysis. Amanda ends her essay about her cousin who was adopted from Mexico at the age of eleven with the truism "immigrants are people just like us." Robert, an intellectually curious Mexican-American student, implicitly counters Trump's policy proposal for a border wall, but does not delve any deeper than his call for readers to "remember to build bridges, not walls."

Kamil, meanwhile, writing about his family's experience coming from Russia, similarly resorts to ending with a weak call for everyone to just get along. He recounts his father's story of struggling for better wages in the construction industry here and describes his father's frustration in losing money to wage theft. But his ending is a tangle of platitudes. "I think we can all work toward into more equalize minded society" and a "better world for everyone," he writes. Straying far from the specifics of his father's tale, Kamil concludes by saying, "This world will outlast all of us so therefore we should be fair and should be open among each other for better transparency."

Despite coaxing from us in classroom discussions and through verbal and written feedback on multiple drafts and often even by classmates working together with them as peer reviewers, these students resisted applying an analytical frame to the personal, to situating their family members' experiences within a political, economic, or historical context. Rather than writing stories that countered or expanded the hegemonic narrative, these students held tightly to the American Dream, even when the evidence did not entirely, or even mostly, point in that direction.

Pattern #2: Complex Tales, Lack of Analysis

Both of us also note how, even when our students are telling rich and complicated personal narratives, they often find it hard not to slide back into pat formulations when they try to make the move away from *telling* these tales to *analyzing* them. Analysis is always difficult, of course. It is challenging for scholars at any level to land on genuinely interesting ideas about the meaning of the material they are studying, and equally challenging to put such ideas in writing. This is particularly true for our students, for whom such an analytical mode is generally unfamiliar. This is, of course, the critique made by many who believe personal writing has little place in an academic setting (Bartholomae). However, we sense, too, that students may hesitate to claim the sort of authority that the analysis we are asking of them demands, an authority that, we acknowledge, presumes a set of rights and privileges to make meaning of one's own and others' tales. So when our students tell a rich story but then stop short of assigning it an equally rich meaning, it is sometimes as though they are asking who are they, after all, to define the meaning of their father's story, or their mother's, or even their own? At other times, it seems that to deeply analyze a tale of familial hardship would be tantamount to admitting personal defeat in the face of a tidal wave of immigration mythology to the contrary.

Libby's student Marissa, for example, recounts a complicated story of coming to the United States from Georgetown, Guyana. Her essay's central question is why people would make the decision to come to the United States, even when they don't have to. She is critical of US culture, seeing it as overly materialistic and shallow. She loved her life in Guyana, where she had friends, romance, and plans for schooling. But she recognizes that her father had a different experience. He would have been heartbroken to stay. He had grown up in a large family that was too poor for him to realize his ambition to be a doctor; instead he wound up working for the electricity company. As he got older, Marissa explains, going to "Americah" became the focus of her father's dreams. She eloquently evokes his yearning: "He wanted to see the snow, he wanted to try the food, he wanted to see the statue of liberty and most of all he wanted to live the illusory good life," she writes. When the two of them were approved for visas to the United States, he was overjoyed. Marissa captures the depth of the divide between her and her father's experience of migration: "On the plane ride over to New York, I cried almost the entire way. My father however looked so happy and excited he was practically glowing. We were stark opposites during this entire transaction. For him this was his was his oldest dream come true but for me it was my worst nightmare."

But Marissa avoids exploring this contradiction any further. Rather, it seems critical to her to conclude by erasing it altogether. She ends her essay on an upbeat note at odds with her story of how her experience and her father's had always clashed:

> My dad's dream . . . took me away from my mother and brother, family and friends that I love but from here I can make them proud. The best part about migrating here was watching my dad, because he came here, as old as he was, got his GED, got his driver's license and finally attained a college diploma after decades of dreaming. Overall, I believe my dad is the true image of American opportunities and I couldn't be prouder of him.

This pat ending was surprising for Libby to read not only because of its departure from the essay's theme of wrenching disagreement, but also because Marissa spent the semester noting, at every turn, the many ways that immigrants' hopes were often thwarted by the economic, legal, racial, and cultural barriers they encountered. Marissa's concluding words might just represent a hasty attempt to tie up the narrative threads, but perhaps they also reflect a reluctance to risk a harder-hitting analysis, for any number of reasons. She might not have wanted to be seen as too harshly condemning her father's actions, or to delve too deeply into her own sadness. Still, the abrupt turn to the tidy ending forecloses on more interesting intellectual work she might have done here, had she explored more fully the ways that migration has often affected different family members differently, or burdened children in ways different from parents.

Vanessa, a Caribbean immigrant student in Emily's class, also presents a complicated view of her coworker's life in the United States after she overstays her visa and is forced to put in long hours for low pay as a nanny while separated from her own children left behind in Trinidad. Vanessa is quick to recognize, both in class and in her written profile, that "things aren't what they seem, in movies or on television shows.

Everyone thinks the grass is greener on the other side especially as an immigrant living in the United States . . . [but] when you don't have any legal status it's harder to find a job in order to maintain life here. You have to do anything that comes your way, even if it pays little to nothing." Yet, rather than delve deeply into the complex issues of race, class, gender, and immigration status that this common immigrant experience for Caribbean women raises, she retreats from any analysis of Stephanie's life, citing the old adage "when life gives you lemons you make lemonade." Vanessa ends her essay with the following generalities about immigrant hard work and fortitude:

> Stephanie's story taught me the power of perseverance; no matter how bleak or daunting a situation may be, you should put in dedicated effort towards achieving your goals. Stephanie made this decision initially with the intentions of making a better life for her children and herself, and no matter how many speed bumps she faced along the way she stuck to her goal until she achieved it.

Perhaps Vanessa is speaking vicariously for herself and her own aspirations when she resorts to repeating these clichés.

Several students in Emily's class chose to write about their undocumented parents. Their lengthy depictions of parental struggle—often to achieve a better life for their children—could easily be read as deeply poignant counter-stories. Yet, despite all the evidence they illustrate in their profiles—and the unfettered vilification of undocumented immigrants in the news—many of these students still chose to hold the dominant immigrant narrative close, ending their profiles on notes of hope and admiration. A DACA recipient from Jamaica, Delyse, gives her profile about her undocumented mother the provocative title, "It Remains to be Seen," implying that the jury is still out on her mother's decision to migrate. Her essay details the many trials her mom has gone through to find adequate housing, gainful employment, and a non-abusive life partner. But Delyse still concludes on a somewhat upbeat note, despite the fact that her mom has a serious medical condition, is uninsured, and struggles to fund her daughter's college education, making Delyse's return to college the following semester uncertain. She writes, "Being an immigrant in the US is challenging at times but it also showed me that they are willing to do anything to survive in America. [My mother] didn't let her immigration status stop her from succeeding in life. My mother's experience taught me that she is a fighter who never gives [up] no matter what obstacles come her way." While Delyse's portrayal of her mom as a fighter seems accurate, her characterization of her mom's life in the United States as successful both seems to contradict the title of her essay and the deep concerns Delyse expressed to Emily about their precarious financial, educational, health, and immigration status.

Effat, a Pakistani immigrant, used her immigrant profile to explore her father's entry into the United States as an undocumented immigrant, the fear and exploitation he suffered in below-minimum-wage jobs, the discrimination he encountered as a Muslim post-9/11, and the fact that he was defrauded by two immigration attorneys in the long, complicated process of obtaining legal status in this country. Though her profile depicts her father as the ultimate immigrant underdog, she too concludes her essay on a positive note, affirming, somewhat inexplicably, that "although Saeed's life was full of hardships however, he never had regret. Saeed was satisfied with his life in US." Though Effat and Delyse seem to welcome the opportunity to document their parents' struggles and to express gratitude for the sacrifices that have been made on their behalf, they retreat from analyzing the odds that are still stacked against their parents and, by extension, themselves. Their reluctance to explicitly acknowledge that their family's immigration experience is anything less than fair, satisfying, and a success shows how deeply rooted our nation's immigration mythology is in their imaginations.

And, finally, Alek, in Libby's class, tells a dramatic and complicated tale of how his family came from Russia and ultimately successfully claimed asylum, but, like Emily's students described above, can't quite follow that tale to an analytically powerful conclusion. He recounts how his father was the first in the family to go to the United States, where he applied for asylum. Alek and his mother, meanwhile, for some reason wound up stranded in Mexico, unable to get documents, and dependent on the kindness of local strangers who put them up. Alek's father jeopardized his pending asylum claim by traveling to Mexico, from where he arranged for all three of them to cross the United States–Mexico border illicitly. Alek's guiding question ("What does it mean to be an asylum seeker?") is a powerful one. But Alek's answer to it, in the end, while not without insight, has a hesitant and partial quality:

> Being an Asylum seeker means having great courage, strength and will power in pursuing a better life, whether it's for family, friends or yourself. Most importantly it means taking a huge risk by becoming vulnerable in trusting strangers with your life in pursuit of happiness. Being an asylum seeker is one of the biggest gambles in life sought out by many and only acquired by few.

Like many of the other students, Alek falls back on a mode of emotional interpretation of the story he tells, leaving untouched many of the important structural questions his story raises about the meaning of national borders, the complexities of immigrants' journeys, and how the workings of immigration law shape families' experiences.

Though we find that many of our students write complicated tales of immigration that *we* read as provocative counter-narratives, rich with links between individual stories and the larger structural forces that shape them, our students often do not seem to see these links clearly themselves. While these students do some kind of analysis in their essays, this analysis remains primarily on the level of the emotional or the personal. Indeed, in these essays, it seems that raising up the specificities and particularities of individual immigrant stories can have the effect of reinforcing, or at least spurring students to reproduce, stereotypical, aspirational immigrant myths because this is what students so badly want to believe for themselves and their loved ones.

Pattern 3: Stories that Speak Back

Nevertheless, the recent turn in our national discourse toward a vilification of undocumented (particularly of Mexican) immigrants is not lost on our students. We have found many instances in which our students situate their stories in relation to the current political assault on immigrants and use these stories to reflect critically on the ways that immigration status, national origin, and US government policies make the experiences of certain immigrants more difficult than others. We readily admit that it seems to have been the election of Trump, rather than any pedagogical innovation of ours, that has inspired such "speaking back" to nativist narratives of immigration.

For example, Alexandra, the US-born daughter of Mexican immigrants, spontaneously placed her mother's story in the current political context from the very first draft of her essay. Many paragraphs of her profile focus on how her mother experienced the rhetoric of the presidential campaign and Trump's subsequent election:

> Being from Mexico, the 2016 presidential election was something that really touched Lupe. She remembered watching Donald Trump announce his candidacy to the presidency, along with openly discriminating against Mexicans. As he stood behind a podium with one of his many long red ties he claimed that "When Mexico sends its people, they're not sending their best. They're not sending you. They're not sending you. They're sending people that have lots of problems, and they're bringing those problems with them. They're bringing drugs. They're bringing crime. They're rapists. And some, I assume, are good people."

Alexandra's essay describes the disillusionment the election sparked in her mother and how it caused her to re-evaluate her own understanding of the position of immigrants in the country where she has lived and raised her children for several decades. Alexandra writes that "[Lupe] didn't think that the place that had provided her with opportunities could elect a man who labeled her entire family as people who were 'bringing drugs,' 'bringing crime,' and claiming them to be 'rapists,' for president but to her dismay on election night he won." Speaking through her mother, Alexandra explicitly connects Trump's election to her mother's rejection of an "immigrants are welcome" mythology, arguing that "the place [Lupe] called home for 28 years, longer than the time she spent in her native country, made her feel like she was no longer welcome. Not only did she feel unwelcome she felt insulted and racially profiled as a criminal who had come to harm the U.S." Alexandra implicitly acknowledges the porosity and fragility of immigration status and the absurdity of the good/bad (documented/undocumented) immigrant dichotomy promulgated by our current administration. Her essay reads as a protest against the erasure of her mother's multi-dimensional humanity:

> Even now as a U.S. resident a part of her feels like everything she went through for her family, her future had now caused others to label her a criminal, to cast aside that she was a mother, a wife, an immigrant who didn't live off the government, who paid taxes, but as someone who simply committed a crime.

For Alexandra, the immigrant profile was a space in which to validate her mother's beliefs and experiences as she spoke back powerfully to Trump's attempt to demonize undocumented Mexicans.

Alek, the Russian student who writes about his family's complicated journey to the United States via Mexico and their effort to gain asylum, may not be fully able to unpack or analyze all the ways that his family's story illuminates the larger workings of US immigration law, but he certainly *points* to them. One of the most compelling moments of his essay comes when he describes his family's experience crossing clandestinely into the United States from Mexico, and then being stopped by US Border Patrol agents:

> The officers ironically thought we were an American family that got lost on vacation and were going to let us go but, they soon realized that we were immigrants due to my mother's lack of English. Border patrol took us to their post. . . . After a few hours of daunting interrogations, we ended up being released and my mother was given a court summons to appear before a judge to determine her eligibility of staying in the country. . . . The officers were surprisingly very kind and helpful.

Alek's inclusion of the detail that the Border Patrol initially took them to be an "American family . . . on vacation," together with his subsequent observation that many Central Americans whose entrance into the country were similar to his own have been denied asylum over the decades, suggests his sensitivity to just how much race and nationality seems to have structured this encounter with the Border Patrol. To be sure, his parents were subjected to "daunting interrogations," but Alek's sense of the "irony" of the situation reflects an understanding that immigration enforcement in the US borderlands is designed primarily to control the migration of Mexicans and Central Americans. Although he never quite spells it out, his narrative points to the way that a white, Russian family—however lost, and however surreptitious their entry into the nation—reads to law enforcement as "American," while those who look or sound to law enforcement like Mexicans or Central Americans are more likely to come under suspicion as unauthorized "aliens," whatever their citizenship or immigration status.

Pattern 4: Placing Stories in Conversation with Published Texts

There are moments in both of our classes, in our end-of-semester projects, in which students do seem able to articulate complicated ideas about how individual immigrant lives are shaped by, and illustrate, powerful social and political forces. In so doing, students capture far more nuanced narratives of immigration, going beyond "American dream" stories, or purely psychological or personal analyses, to teach their reader something important about the complexities and contradictions of immigration. For Emily, this often happens in the context of the research essays with which her students end the semester, drawing on texts the class has read (Valeria Luiselli's *Tell Me How It Ends: An Essay in Forty Questions* and Cristina Henríquez's *The Book of Unknown Americans*) as well as independent research to produce a position paper on some aspect of immigration. Though these assignments might seem to invite a sort of writing quite distant from the personal narratives with which students start the semester, Emily finds that the most compelling of her students' research papers grow out of questions raised by the narratives and represent a recognition that personal and political experience are intertwined.

Students' stories resonate strongly in their essay questions, yet many are able to embrace a more critical vision of immigration in their research essays, precisely because they have to rely on more than their own personal experiences and aspirations to support their claims. Thus, we found that when we blurred the artificial divide between personal and academic writing—a divide that compositionists have discussed and debated over the past few decades—our students achieved their best writing. Allowing personal stories of migration into our curricula led students to genuine questions that, in turn, lent themselves to embracing a form of argument-based writing that is more commonly associated with college-level composition and history classes.

For example, Jada, a Mongolian immigrant from Russia, wrote a powerful, meticulously researched essay on how cultural misunderstandings can negatively impact the outcome of asylum petitions. She drew from our course text, her own independent research, and her personal knowledge of fellow Russians who had fled ethnic discrimination in Russia, like the friend she profiled at the start of the semester. Her essay argues that "thousands of asylum applicants are deported back to their home countries every year. Difference[s] in culture, which cause different understanding of many things, influence on the outcome of asylum process." Jada delves into a host of scholarly articles to show how an immigrant's nonchronological narrative style, inability to distinguish personal from political persecution, or lack of emotional affect when describing traumatic events clashes with the rigid, culturally biased expectations of the asylum process. Jada not only argues in favor of a more culturally competent asylum process, but she implicitly critiques the xenophobia inherent in US immigration policy, advocating for an expansive view of asylum seekers and refugees as "a part of an American society." Influenced by Luiselli's depiction of the plight of Central American unaccompanied minors as they journey through US immigration courts, Jada argues that we should not "see their [refugees or asylum seekers'] problems as foreign problems" but, rather, that we should "treat migrant children's problems as local ones." She ends her essay with the affirmation that the United States has the moral responsibility to welcome and support refugees and asylum seekers, stating simply that, "it should be a norm to help them." In this final essay, Jada takes a transnational leap in the telling of immigrant stories, moving from a personal tale of ethnic persecution in Russia to a critical analysis of the asylum process in the country she has begun to call home.

Safiya chose to write her research essay about the undocumented parents of US citizen children, a question that piqued her interest precisely because of her own experience of familial separation. Safiya's mother left Egypt due to the stigma associated with divorce and her inability to support her daughters as a single mom. When she overstayed her tourist visa she lived in New York for six years as an undocumented immigrant,

unable to visit her daughters, without any family support during chemo-
therapy after a serious cancer diagnosis. Safiya's profile of her mother
details these hardships, yet she ends with the truly surprising assessment
that "the *fair* life in America makes the immigrants satisfied about their
living here" (emphasis ours).

The distancing lens of research seemed to allow Safiya to take a more
critical view of US policy toward undocumented immigrants. Safiya begins
her research essay with the unequivocal statement, "Undocumented
parents of U.S. citizen-children should not be deported." She goes on
to explain:

> In the United States, there are a lot of families that have the same issue, the
> parents are undocumented and the children are U.S. citizens. According
> to a survey about these families, there's an article shows that "The number
> of children in mixed status families is estimated to be around 9 million,
> about 4 million of whom are U.S.-born citizens."

Safiya discovers, in the scholarly articles she consults to write her essay,
that what she had thought was simply a personal story, is actually the
experience of "a huge number" of families whom, she argues, "we cannot neglect or don't care too much [about] considering them as families
from the second class." In this essay, she reconsiders her mother's undocumented immigration status and reframes what she had previously
considered a personally painful, somewhat shameful family secret as a
social and political problem of epic proportions. There is power in this
new reading of her family's experience, shaped by knowledge she has
gleaned from her own research and our course texts. Safiya harnesses
her own experiences as a motherless adolescent, armed with newfound
evidence, to cogently argue against current US immigration policy:
"Nine million . . . U.S. children, of course they should have their right to
be with their families in their country America."

Libby's students, meanwhile, also do sometimes succeed at putting
the personal in conversation with the structural. Like Emily's students,
they do this best when they are engaging with the texts they studied in
class throughout the semester, bringing the work of scholars such as
Kelly Lytle Hernández, Mae Ngai, George Sánchez, and others to bear
on the personal tales they are writing about.

For example, Fatima, a Syrian immigrant, examines the way that contemporary immigrants' experiences with a discriminatory legal system
are part of a much longer historical arc. She chose to interview a Syrian
family friend who came to the United States from Saudi Arabia. The
friend, a pediatrician, described a relatively privileged relationship to

the process of immigration. He was able to secure a US visa and a job at a Brooklyn hospital without too much difficulty. Nevertheless, he shared with Fatima some of the insecurity that he felt as a Syrian immigrant in the face of widespread prejudice and the Trump administration's new policies, particularly its travel ban, which left him uncertain of whether he would be permitted to reenter the United States were he to leave. In her commentary on this interview, Fatima explores the idea "that the fear of deportation and insecurities felt by immigrants from certain Muslim minority countries today is similar to the insecurities felt by certain immigrant groups in the past, especially the Asian Americans." She describes the long history of US policy defining Asians as permanent outsiders—long largely banned from both immigration and citizenship, from the time of the Chinese Exclusion Act of 1882 through the mid-twentieth century. She also connects her interviewee's experiences in airports, where he described being subject to special scrutiny, not only to the ways that Asians have been historically marked as threatening outsiders, but also to the experiences of Mexican immigrants, who came to be regarded with particular suspicion on the nation's southern border as the US border-guarding regime evolved in the early twentieth century. "The experiences of immigrants nowadays," Fatima concludes, "have many similarities to the experiences of immigrants in the last two hundred years, where certain groups of individuals are treated less than others based on their national origin and race."

Ahmed, meanwhile, wrote a thoughtful essay that cast insight in the opposite direction, using his family story as a lens to more fully understand the decision-making processes of the historical actors we had studied. In his piece, Ahmed explores the question of why people decide to leave their homes, a question that had deep personal meaning for him. He delves first into his father's decision to immigrate from Yemen to the United States, leaving Ahmed's mother and his older siblings—Ahmed was not born until later—behind in a place wracked by both war and economic upheaval. It was many months before the family heard from Ahmed's father, who was ashamed to find himself struggling in New York City, unable to send money or secure visas. Finally, he did both, and the family reunited. Ahmed had long wondered about how his father could, even temporarily, abandon his family so completely. In his essay, he muses about the answer to his question that arises from his father's experience:

> I came to understand that my dad had two choices and both options were [rich with] sadness and crisis. Staying was a crisis and leaving was also a crisis. Coming to the U.S. paid off eventually, but there were costs.

> My siblings were angry and blamed him for leaving them behind, even
> though they came to understand the reasons why they decided to move.

In the writing that follows this passage, Ahmed considers the history
of other immigrants through this lens of his father's experience. In
particular, he attends closely to the ways that many people's decisions
to migrate, whether from Morocco, the Philippines, or elsewhere,
must be understood in the context of crisis, particularly "economic
change, or upheavals," that they are facing at home. He concludes
that "people have choices," but that "we can also see why they make
the choices they do." People have agency, in other words, but agency
within limits—limits often determined by harsh economic conditions
and other kinds of upheaval.

THE BRIDGE TO SOCIAL JUSTICE: MOVING FROM THE
CLASSROOM TO THE COLLEGE AND BEYOND

Our teaching and curricula grow out of our political as well as our scholarly and pedagogical commitments. Both of us are engaged, on our campus and beyond, with larger struggles for immigrant justice, from the
sanctuary campus movement, to work with asylum-seekers and neighborhood organizing. However, we often find it challenging to balance our
deep political convictions with what happens in our classrooms and on
our campus. Immediately following the 2016 presidential elections, a
number of faculty and students on our campus joined together to support sanctuary campus and immigrants' rights initiatives. Like activists
at other colleges around the country, we pressed our administration
to declare Kingsborough a sanctuary campus. These efforts met with
limited success. We were able to extract certain specific promises (such
as increased resources for legal aid to immigrant students, measures to
safeguard student data, instructions to college security not to contact or
question students on the basis of immigration status) from our administration. But, like the administrations at the other City University of New
York colleges, Kingsborough's institutional leaders stopped short of an
emphatic declaration of sanctuary for undocumented students. This
organizing in support of immigrant students, and particularly undocumented immigrant students, was more contentious than we might have
expected in our deeply blue, overwhelmingly immigrant city. Moving
out of our classrooms into college-wide conversations often felt as if we
were swimming against the current of our own pedagogical practices
and curricular goals. Ironically, our campus-based organizing initiatives

led us to realize that our college administration clung to its own version of pat narratives about immigrant students (We are a city and campus of immigrants! Everyone is welcome here! Everyone can succeed if they work hard!) without being willing to craft new policy or allocate additional resources to protect undocumented and other noncitizen students in this era of heightened immigration enforcement. Ultimately, our efforts to create a robust student-faculty-staff working group on immigration fell apart when the administrative members of the committee announced that they were just too busy to continue to meet.

Many students, including some who had first discussed their own immigration stories and the broader context of immigration policies in our own classrooms, were passionate about the issues the sanctuary campus organizing raised, and a dedicated core of students has continued to work on flyering, know-your-rights events, and other immigrant rights' initiatives. But it has proven difficult to sustain mass participation in these initiatives in an ongoing way, especially once the immediate post-election fear and anxiety simmered down. Though students were eager, for example, to attend a meeting with the administration in order to resolve a particular issue they experienced on campus, such as discrimination against undocumented students in the financial aid office, most were quickly overwhelmed by the demands of day-to-day life, and organizing for institutional change took a back seat. As commuter students who go to school full-time, work many hours each week, and shoulder a host of family responsibilities, this is unfortunate though not surprising ("Public Scholars"). Given that our administration did not welcome faculty and student organizing to influence college policy in support of immigrant students, it has been challenging, to say the least, to maintain students' enthusiasm for this work.

Furthermore, it has not always been easy to connect our campus organizing to our classrooms in an organic way. Despite the fact that teaching immigrant stories seems entirely relevant to our community college context, building bridges to social justice can prove elusive. We stubbornly hold to the conviction that it is not for us to visualize or define what social justice would look like for our students. In fact, our deepest pedagogical beliefs dictate that any social justice action would have to grow out of students' own analyses, desires, and convictions, and take a form that they would imagine for themselves. Though we design our curricula and make the pedagogical choices described above with these thoughts and goals in mind, it is clearly not in our control whether, when, or how students embrace a vision of immigrant stories as a bridge to social justice.

At the same time, as scholars, we are committed to the idea that there is deep intellectual value in working toward a kind of analysis that links the macro with the micro, the personal with the political, larger social forces with the smaller ones that structure people's lives. We believe that there is a kind of social justice embedded in working with students to develop such analyses, even if it's a reach for them that they don't quite make while they are in our classes, or at our college. We hope at the least that we are modeling the kind of thinking that we do as scholars and activists as well as teachers. We study and teach about those links because we believe that in order to understand the trials and travails of real people, you need to understand the larger forces at play: the discourse, and the laws and policies around immigration that shape and constrain so many of our students' and their families' lives and fortunes. We teach immigrant stories because they are real stories with real stakes for real people.

Finally, we would like to close with a final thought about how we hope that working with our students on writing about immigrant stories "speaks back" to the current political moment. The Trump administration did not invent neoliberal educational imperatives any more than it invented a punitive immigration enforcement regime. But those imperatives—like the immigration enforcement regime—have only gotten more extreme under the current administration and seem to be here to stay. Humanities departments are under siege, the value of teaching subjects like literature and history is in doubt. Like other beleaguered educational institutions, particularly public ones, community colleges are subject to increasing political scrutiny and ever-harsher funding constraints. We face intense pressure to produce better "outcomes" at all costs. We are told that what matters most is cost efficiency, graduation rates, and market-oriented skills training. In this context of austerity and fundamental mistrust of our disciplines, we believe that the teaching and telling of immigrant stories represents a measure of resistance. Teaching immigrant stories has become, sadly, a radical project. We believe that telling the stories of our classrooms—and the messy, complicated, incomplete teaching and learning that happens within them—is vital at this moment when reductive educational policies prevail. We hope that this chapter contributes, in however modest a way, to this political enterprise. Telling *our* stories of teaching immigrant stories—stories of students like Yuliya, Marissa, Jada, Alek, Effat, Kamil, Fatima, and the others whose work we explore here—is one way, we hope, to make a case for the kinds of reading, writing, and learning that we believe matter, that preserve spaces where students are not merely regarded as customers or future employees, but as historical, speaking and writing subjects, empowered to construct their own narratives about the forces that structure their lives.

WORKS CITED

Bartholomae, David. "Writing with Teachers: A Conversation with Peter Elbow." *College Composition and Communication*, vol. 46, no. 1, 1995, pp. 62–71.

Bloom, Lynn Z. "That Way Be Monsters: Myths and Bugaboos about Teaching Personal Writing." Annual CCCC Convention, 13 Apr. 2000, Minneapolis.

Elbow, Peter. "Reflections on Academic Discourse: How It Relates to Freshman and Colleagues." *College English*, vol. 53, 1991, pp. 135–155.

Fontaine, Sheryl I., and Susan Hunter. *Writing Ourselves into the Story: Unheard Voices from Composition Studies.* Southern Illinois UP, 1993.

Hernández, Kelly Lytle. *City of Inmates: Conquest, Rebellion, and the Rise of Human Caging in Los Angeles, 1771–1965.* The University of North Carolina Press, 2017.

Kimball, Elizabeth, et al. "Writing the Personal in an Outcomes-Based World." *Composition Studies*, vol. 43, no. 2, Fall 2015, pp. 113–131.

Luiselli, Valeria. *Tell Me How It Ends: An Essay in Forty Questions.* Coffee House Press, 2017.

"National Origin (Degree Students Only)." *Kingsborough Community College Institutional Research*, Fall 2016, https://www.kbcc.cuny.edu/irap/documents/IP2016/Page4.pdf.

Ngai, Mae. "The Architecture of Race in American Immigration Law: A Reexamination of the Immigration Act of 1924." *The Journal of American History*, vol. 86, no. 1, 1999, pp. 67–92.

Rose, Mike. *Lives on the Boundary.* Penguin Books, 1989.

Sánchez, George J. *Becoming Mexican American: Ethnicity, Culture and Identity in Chicano Los Angeles, 1900–1945.* Oxford University Press, 1993.

Sánchez, S. A. "From the Public Scholars: Students' Experiences, Embodiments, and Enactments of Civic Engagement at KCC." *Brooklyn Public Scholars Evaluation.* Public Science Project, City University of New York Graduate Center, 2014.

Spigelman, Candace. "Argument and Evidence in the Case of the Personal." *College English*, vol. 64, no. 1, Sept. 2001, pp. 63–87.

Spigelman, Candace. *Personally Speaking: Experience as Evidence in Academic Discourse.* SIUP, 2004.

8

TEACHING IMMIGRATION IN A WRITING-INTENSIVE HONORS COURSE

John C. Havard, Silvia Giagnoni, Timothy J. Henderson, Brennan Herring, and Rachel Pate

In fall 2017 we co-taught a junior research seminar on immigration through Auburn University at Montgomery's (AUM) University Honors Program (UHP). The course, HONR3757, is an open-topic seminar that includes a research project that should prepare students to write their honors theses ("Honors Courses"). Immigration is an ideal topic for such a course. First of all, the course must be interdisciplinary and could be team-taught to that end. Only by examining immigration's various historical, social, and cultural contexts can the topic be understood. We joined forces to teach the topic in these lights: Silvia Giagnoni works on contemporary Alabama's anti-immigrant political climate and the stories of immigrants living in the state; John C. Havard on US literature and Anglo-American Hispanophobia; and Timothy J. Henderson on historical factors in Mexico that have led to patterns of migration to the United States. Together, we developed a course that exposed students to the history of US immigration, the media's representation of immigrants, and how literature complicates the topic.

Immigration was also useful for creating a strong course in research writing. To engage the topic, students must navigate often-unreliable information disseminated in polarized public discourses. The debates to which they respond have real-world consequences. In doing so, they must develop information-literacy skills and consider the implications of their work. Moreover, the challenge of engaging a topic of such consequence stimulates commitment to inquiry.

We also developed the course because immigration is responsive to UHP's Global Citizenship outcomes, which pertain to becoming more open-minded; developing understanding of the relationships between the global and the local; and approaching enduring problems equitably

https://doi.org/10.7330/9781646421664.c008

("UHP Outcomes Rubric"). Global economic and political disruptions continue to spur migration, and the US anti-immigrant movement has been invigorated by the 2016 election results. In this climate, immigration and immigrant rights have become one of our society's most pressing equity issues. This is true both nationally and on our students' local level as inhabitants of a Deep South state in which immigration has spiked in recent decades, spurring virulent anti-immigrant backlash. We devised the course hoping that the topic's ethically and emotionally challenging dimensions—which involve tensions over US national identity as well as immigrants' compelling human stories—would provoke transformative reflection that motivates not just an invested writing process but also dedication to building a just global society.

This essay describes our course units and assignments, the ways the course succeeded, and what we wish we had done differently. We highlight the experiences of two students, Brennan Herring and Rachel Pate, who describe how the course challenged them to improve their writing processes, analytical skills, and commitments to equity. We hope the essay will provide useful resources and cautionary tales for faculty with similar aims.

OVERARCHING ELEMENTS OF THE COURSE

We divided the course into three units, each led by Drs. Giagnoni, Havard, or Henderson based on area of expertise: one on history, one on media, and one on literature. The course also featured three overarching assignments: a current events scrapbook, an interview with an immigrant or an individual who works closely with immigrants, and a research project based on a question the student developed from the interview. We asked students to develop research projects connected to their major and/or career aspirations. We also encouraged two co-curricular activities, a UHP forum discussion organized in conjunction with our course, and visitations with detainees at the Stewart Detention Center.

The current events scrapbook required students to find a single article each week on a topic concerning immigration. With help from AUM's library staff, we prepared students by coaching them on information literacy and how to assess sources on immigration for accuracy. We also taught students how to use online aggregators and databases to search for such articles.

We included this assignment because we wanted students to hone their information-literacy skills by thinking carefully about the representation of immigration and immigrants in the media. We also wanted them to immerse themselves in the issue's rapidly evolving political, legal, and media climate. They would then, we hoped, be able to relate what they learned about immigration's historical, media, and literary contexts to current events. We encouraged students to make such connections by devoting time at the beginning of some of our classes to discussing what they were learning. These discussions did not always go as planned: some discussions veered off topic in problematic ways, perhaps to be expected in a class dealing with a topic about which students have strong but poorly informed opinions. At other times, students seemed overwhelmed by competing expectations of finding articles for their scrapbooks, preparing for the disciplinary unit of the day, and making connections between the two. At these times, discussion faltered. However, at their best, these discussions provided opportunities for students to pool information; make connections to the history, media, and literature units; as well as to practice information-literacy skills by offering us opportunities to correct misinformation they encountered. We hoped this process would drive home the topic's importance and nuances. We also assumed students would have no trouble finding a wealth of consequential material to report on—and indeed, fall 2017 provided endless storylines. Moreover, some students, particularly those who made connections with DACA recipients, were able to meaningfully incorporate current events into the research projects they built from their interviews.

The course's second overarching element was an assignment to interview an immigrant or someone who works closely with immigrants. With our consultation, students arranged interviews and produced transcripts. We designed this assignment with two goals in mind. First of all, to supplement Dr. Giagnoni's discussion of her book *Here We May Rest*, we hoped students would connect with and learn more about immigration in our local Montgomery, Alabama community. UHP's Global Citizenship outcome emphasizes understanding relationships between local and global trends. The scrapbook assignment was geared toward national and global storylines. The interview, though, would help students engage local matters. Inhibiting the assignment's effectiveness was that many students did not stray far from the familiar in conducting their interviews. For instance, a few interviewed AUM faculty. Others interviewed fellow students. One interviewed a family friend. However, many students gained meaningful knowledge about immigration's local dimensions. Some learned about which professions local immigrants work in. Two students, who interviewed an AUM faculty member from the College of Education who is both an immigrant and an advocate, were moved by this professor's passion for supporting the immigrant community. Rachel Pate, who shares her experiences below, interviewed a friend and learned about the psychological burdens of being a DACA recipient in a red state with a history of anti-immigrant sentiment and legislation.

Our second goal for the interviews pertained to the research project. We asked students to identify research questions based on what they learned in the interviews. We assumed that immigration is an emotionally fraught issue and that students would best engage with research if they made a personal connection with an immigrant and listened firsthand to their concerns. As such, research would not just be an academic exercise but an effort to find evidence-based solutions to real human problems affecting our community. Although many students conducted compelling interviews, whether those conversations yielded fruitful research projects was a mixed bag. Rachel, the student who interviewed a DACA recipient, designed a superb research project on immigrants' experience of stress and trauma. She had probed the interviewee for traumatic experiences both prior to, during, and after immigrating; the conversation particularly dwelt on the interviewee's experience of hope and improved opportunities when DACA was instituted; of fear, depression, and diminished academic performance when the Trump administration announced that DACA would be phased out; and of anger at racially charged insults levied against the interviewee in the community. Rachel designed a project of further investigating psychological studies speaking to experiences of trauma and stress experienced by immigrants prior to, during, and after immigration. The paper concluded that immigration-specific trauma assessments are needed. The project was focused and well-researched, and the paper was written effectively. It successfully used research in psychological studies regarding immigrants' experiences to demonstrate the stark human reality of struggle with PTSD that underlies dehumanizing right-wing representations of immigrants as invaders. Moreover, the student's interview and research process involved a galvanizing experience of developing a greater commitment to equity that lead the student to develop a solution to a real human problem. However, other students struggled to capitalize on leads gained during their interviews. For instance, one student who interviewed an immigrant from an East Asian country designed a history project on immigration to the United States from that country. The project initially seemed promising, and the paper made good use of statistical research to identify broad trends on the issue. However, the student failed to follow up on Dr. Henderson's suggestion to include illustrative

personal narratives to provide a human dimension to the historical analysis. As the example illustrates, some students struggled to devote the
necessary time to produce stellar research writing. This challenge was
likely exacerbated by an overly ambitious course.

The last overarching assignment was the research paper itself. Based
on a question they developed from their interview, students were to
conduct scholarly research and to write a relatively short paper of five
to six pages on their findings. Ideally, because the UHP's curriculum
is designed for this project to prepare students to write their senior
theses, the paper was to develop a solution to a problem pertinent to
their major or career aspirations. Some students were very successful in
developing research topics from their interviews that were clearly connected to their majors. A case in point was a communications disorders
major who interviewed the aforementioned education faculty member.
This professor is very active in the immigrant community; he taught
immigrant students for years at a local K–12 institution prior to entering academia, and he still personally tutors them. Our student talked
to him about how education professionals often treat these students
like they have a speech disorder when they are really struggling with
language acquisition and assimilating. In light of this discussion, they
addressed the faculty member's views on whether bilingual education
should be practiced in the schools. Based on their conversation, the
student designed a project on bilingual education. He discussed the
history of divisive debate regarding these programs; compared models;
and particularly related, in light of research in communication disorders, potential benefits of bilingual programs for students with hearing
loss or speech impairment. The paper made proposals for educational
policy based on these findings. In addition to being well-researched
and well-written, the resultant paper exemplified the goal for students
to build off the interview and develop solutions to important problems
studied in their disciplines, not to mention our broader goals of utilizing
the research process to develop awareness of diversity and to encourage
equity. However, not all students achieved this level of success.

The course also featured two co-curricular events. Students were
encouraged to participate in these events and were assessed for whether
or not they did so as part of a participation score; those who were unable
to participate could make up the participation points via other means.
The first event was a panel discussion organized by AUM UHP director
Matthew Jordan. Our hope was that, by participating in the forum, our
students would be further exposed to the kinds of people involved in
debates regarding immigration and the positions they take. The panel

discussed the question, "What I wish everyone understood about immigration." The event was part of a series of such discussions organized by Dr. Jordan. The series' purpose is to encourage civil discussion of polarizing topics. For instance, previously, a human rights activist and a law professor at a conservative Christian university debated whether "religious liberty" laws constitute unjust discrimination. The events are widely advertised and well attended by local community members and AUM students, faculty, and staff. At the immigration forum, panelists were given five to seven minutes to state their positions. After all the panelists had spoken, they debated each other and took audience questions. The speakers were Nicolas Bartell, director of the Montgomery Field Office of the United States Citizenship and Immigration Services (USCIS); Sam McLure, a candidate for Alabama attorney general; Cesar Mata, of Adelante Alabama Worker Center; Jessica Vosburgh, staff attorney for the National Day Laborer Organizing Network and director of the Alabama Worker's Center; and Alan Cross, a local pastor and representative of the National Immigration Forum. The lineup was chosen to present attendees with occupational and ideological diversity. Bartell declined to comment on the ideological dimensions of immigration and instead discussed his observations as a USCIS attorney overseeing immigrants' experiences navigating the naturalization system. McLure, a conservative Alabama Republican, defended his restrictionist perspectives by attempting to square Biblical precepts that seem to support kindness toward immigrants with other Biblical passages that he argued suggest that we should prioritize protecting our families. Mata, an immigrant and community organizer, combatted stereotypes of immigrants propagated by the conservative media by discussing his observations of immigrants' efforts to achieve the American Dream. Vosburgh critiqued investment in border enforcement and US economic and military activity overseas, both of which she argued spur rather than limit immigration. Cross, a social conservative who has developed a progressive view on immigration, detailed his transition from being a typical white Southern evangelical to believing that white Southern Christians had historically been on the wrong side of civil rights issues. These statements were followed by a lively discussion of various topics, for instance whether HB56 had caused post-traumatic stress syndrome in local immigrants. Several of our students attended, and in the following class we reflected on what was discussed.

The second co-curricular event was a trip to El Refugio and the Stewart Detention Center in Lumpkin, Georgia. In conjunction with the aforementioned goals of inspiring research and global citizenship,

we hoped this visit would provide students with more intimate exposure to the unjust practices of the US immigration detention system.
Stewart is one of the largest detention facilities in the country with
a two-thousand-inmate capacity. The for-profit corporation that runs
Stewart was formerly called Corrections Corporation of America and has
now rebranded with the seemingly innocuous name CoreCivic. Stewart
has its own adjoining immigration court, and it has one of the country's
highest denial rates. Called "the black hole of America's immigration
system" in a *Vice* exposé published in collaboration with the Marshall
Project, Stewart is notorious in the immigrant justice movement for its
deplorable conditions (Thompson). El Refugio is a nonprofit, volunteer-
operated hospitality house that offers services to detainees and their
families, including arranging for humanitarian visitation to detainees
and providing a free place to stay for their visiting families ("About El
Refugio"). Through the leadership of Dr. Giagnoni, who had previously
volunteered with El Refugio, we arranged to be given an informational
meeting at El Refugio to learn about its ministry, about Stewart's history,
and the conditions in the facility. Lumpkin, Georgia is a two-hour drive
from our campus's location in Montgomery. As such, visiting was an
all-day affair that we conducted on a Saturday in October and, regret-
tably, only one of our students was able to commit. Several other AUM
students who were not in our class visited through our SPLC on-campus
chapter, which worked with us to organize its trip. After arriving, a vol-
unteer with El Refugio provided the informational session. El Refugio
advertises its presence to detainees in the facility, who can request a
visitation. Students took part in this ministry, getting to know detainees
who came to the United States for opportunity or to escape conditions
in their home countries but who are now languishing in substandard
conditions. The experience spurred the students' concern for the injustice faced by such individuals. Perhaps not coincidentally, the student
from our class who came, Rachel, is the same one who wrote an excel-
lent research paper on the traumas immigrants experience.

HISTORY UNIT, BY TIMOTHY J. HENDERSON

Our honors class on American immigration began midway into the
first year of the Trump presidency, a time when the immigration issue
was prominent in the news. As the class began, the administration was
increasing deportations, talking up its plan to build a wall on the southern border, and outlining its scheme for overhauling legal immigration.
Also during this time Trump announced his plan to end Deferred Action

for Childhood Arrivals (DACA), the Obama-era program that gave legal status to immigrants brought into the country illegally as children. Several high-level administration figures were infamous for their nativist views, including political advisor Stephen Miller, attorney general Jeff Sessions, White House advisor Steve Bannon, and the president himself.

Given that future historians will likely look back on the Trump administration as a significant moment in American immigration history, my hope in designing the history section of this team-taught class was to keep students abreast of current developments even as they learned about the key turning points in American immigration history. These turning points include the periodic outbursts of virulent nativism, the passage of restrictionist legislation, shifting attitudes toward refugees and guest workers, the rise of illegal immigration, and ongoing debates about how immigration fits into the murky concept of "American values." My strategy for keeping students abreast of current developments included showing a video, on the first day of class, of a heated exchange between Trump advisor Stephen Miller and CNN reporter Jim Acosta regarding how to interpret America's immigration history. Acosta argued that the United States has traditionally been humane and welcoming toward immigrants, citing the Emma Lazarus poem at the base of the Statue of Liberty as evidence. Miller responded that the poem was added belatedly and did not reflect the intended meaning of the statue, which in his view was to shine a beacon of freedom outward into the world rather than to beckon immigrants to America's shores. The video clip framed the debate starkly, and I hoped that framing would inform the entire class. I reinforced the point by having students read a pair of op-ed pieces that reflected similar stances toward immigration (e.g., Buchanan). And finally, we required students to compile scrapbooks that included one article per week about current developments in immigration, and we periodically opened the floor for discussion of their findings.

In my lectures I sought to develop key, enduring themes in immigration history: concerns about national security; fear of immigrants' impact on the economy (immigrants as job-stealers, public charges, etc.); shifting policies toward refugees and displaced persons; and concerns that immigrants will fail to assimilate to American culture and will ultimately weaken or destroy it; and associations of immigrants—especially undocumented ones—with criminality. Many of these concerns can be lumped under the rubric of "nativism," a topic we examined in its many vicissitudes. I had students read two short books: David Gerber's *American Immigration: A Very Short Introduction*, and my own book, *Beyond Borders:*

A History of Mexican Immigration to the United States (both published in 2011). I also arranged for an appearance (via Skype) of Dr. Cindy Hahamovitch, the author of two award-winning books on guest workers in the United States. Although none of the students in the class were history majors, I hoped to convey to them the essence of historical methodology, that is, the study of continuity and change over time, the importance of context, the responsible use of evidence, and the complex impacts—many unintended—of watershed moments such as the immigration reforms of 1924 and 1965.

Students were required to write an essay about an important aspect of immigration history. I tried to craft questions that would be intriguing and provocative. The questions dealt with the reasons for nativism, the efficacy of guest worker programs, and the impact of the immigration issue on US relations with Mexico. The most consistent criticism I made of the essays was simply that they did not take history sufficiently into account. Indeed, several focused almost exclusively on current situations; one did a decent job of recounting the history of an issue and also discussed contemporary events but did not connect the history to the present day in any meaningful way; one essay was little more than an impassioned rant, bringing up a potential pitfall of courses such as this one, which dealt with a topic that has considerable emotional resonance for some individuals. On balance, it is fair to say that I was largely unsuccessful in my efforts to imbue these students with a solid appreciation of the value of the study of history. On end-of-term evaluations, one student went so far as to opine that the history section of the course consisted mostly of "unnecessary lecturing and reading assignments."

One of the problems, I think, is inherent in the university's Honors Program itself. Students in the program are conditioned to expect that their classes will be unconventional, and they seemed to resent having to sit through what were, admittedly, rather conventional lectures. If I had fully appreciated this beforehand, I would likely have structured the class more around discussions of the readings. I would also have devoted more class time to discussion of the contemporary events students were presumably learning about by compiling their scrapbooks. A hazard of this approach, however, is that discussions in this class had a tendency often to veer wildly off topic. This tendency was so commonplace that the Honors Program director devised an ingenious method for dealing with it called the "parking lot." Topics raised in discussion that seemed interesting but unrelated to the matter at hand were figuratively placed in a "parking lot," to perhaps be revisited at some later time.

MEDIA UNIT, BY SILVIA GIAGNONI

To introduce my media module, I had the students reflect on the importance of media representations, especially on a topic like immigration. Most of our knowledge today is mediated, not firsthand. During the first two to three classes, I introduced several key concepts and theories such as narrative, discourse, cultivation theory, stereotyping, Stuart Hall's idea of representation as constitutive, and Howard Zinn's notion of (direct) contact (Hall; Zinn). I tried to connect the latter to the difficulty students reported in finding someone to interview, which was their first formal assignment for the course. We challenged the students to explore their own family ties to immigrants—one of them, for instance, was a second-generation Palestinian—and mostly to get out of their comfort zone. For the majority of the students who were Caucasian, this meant to question whether their contact with immigrants they knew had been "massive, prolonged, equal, and intimate" (Zinn 92). Only this type of direct (read, firsthand) contact, according to Zinn, enables the necessary meaningful, interpersonal exchange that can lead to social change.

To challenge their own preconceived ideas about immigrants, on the very first day of classes we had students read an op-ed by journalist Héctor Tobar (*Translation Nation, Deep Down Dark*). Tobar aptly calls the monotonous images of Latinx immigrants crossing the border or handcuffed while waiting to be deported "immigration porn." Such portrayals, he argues, are dehumanizing as they capture their subjects "at the most vulnerable and degrading moment in their lives." Tobar questions the repetitive nature of these representations, claiming that they "have accumulated in our collective national consciousness as the essence of the Latino experience." In the absence of real firsthand knowledge, media portrayals end up becoming the primary source of understanding for most; this recurrence of similar images also fosters stereotypes, as we rarely see a Latinx doctor or teacher represented.

We then discussed the importance of language and the (ab)use of the terms "illegal" and "illegality" in the discourses around immigration. This led to a conversation about the conflation of Mexican, illegal, Hispanic, and immigrant in public discourses. We compared such discourses with data about Latinx in the United States from a March 2017 report by the Migration Policy Institute. There are 56.6 million Latinx, which represents 17.6 percent of the population, and 19.5 million of these are immigrants, with 11.6 million being Mexicans (Zong and Batalova).

I also introduced the class to the work of José Antonio Vargas and his Define America project. In this context, we discussed the latest guidelines the Associated Press had adopted in talking about immigration. In 2013 the AP officially recognized that calling immigrants without a US-issued ID "illegal" was diminishing and recommended journalists and media practitioners avoid using the term (Colford). I asked students and the other faculty not to use "illegal" when referring to undocumented immigrants. This proved to be a challenge, which is further evidence of its widespread use in the media and in our culture generally.

In order to further explore the discourse of illegality, I assigned readings from Aviva Chomsky's *Undocumented*, whose purpose is to denaturalize the articulation of illegality in discourses around US immigration. Chomsky also debunks a variety of myths surrounding immigration as well as reframes practices undocumented individuals may engage in while living in the United States, such as "marrying for documents" or using a false Social Security number in order to work. The purpose of looking at larger social and cultural practices places my approach within cultural and media studies. I strive to provide a larger context for how meanings are produced and communicated because "the media," as I tell my students, are not abstract entities that sort effects in a void; rather, they comprise people who make conscious decisions within certain sociohistorical, economic, and political contexts.

We then tackled competing media narratives by looking at the "legalistic discourse of borders" and the "human discourse of personhood" as discussed in Otto Santa Ana's essay, "The Cowboy and the Goddess." I also introduced the class to Leo Chavez's idea of the "Latino Threat Narrative," and we watched excerpts from the Media Education Foundation's video, *Latinos Beyond Reel* (Picker and Sun), which shed a light on the historical misrepresentation of Latinx peoples and its effects on audiences. I supplemented the discussion with data from the report on the Latinx's presence (or, rather, the lack thereof) in the media, *The Latino Media Gap* (Negrón-Muntaner et al.).

Because of my work on Alabama immigrants, I thought it would make sense to localize the issue and inform the class on Alabama and immigration and, more specifically, on HB56, or the Beason-Hammon Alabama Taxpayer and Citizen Protection Act that passed in 2011. Only one student had heard of the bill prior to taking our course, which is in line with the general lack of knowledge I encountered in my research. I prompted the class to discuss the political and social contexts in which HB56 came about, its "anti-illegal immigration" or "anti-immigrant" nature, the role legalism played in the passing/justification of the bill as well as its (implicit) doctrine of self-deportation. We then compared the narratives of immigration found in my book to the ones in the mainstream media; finally, I asked how the Bible had been used to fight or support HB56. The discussion steered toward religion and took a rather philosophical turn, which found us faculty ill-prepared to properly moderate given lack of biblical knowledge. As instructors we reflected on this occurrence and others and concluded that perhaps being in the Deep South affected the conversation whenever it touched on religious issues in unpredictable ways, thus also impinging on the intended purposes of our lesson plans.

Finally, as I described the assignment for my unit, I supplemented the non-immigration specific information literacy sessions with the librarians with an overview on sources and specifically on the major organizations that produce reports and studies on immigration—Cato Institute, the Center for Immigration Studies, NumbersUSA, and Migration Policy Institute.

For my unit assignment, students were required to perform a three-to-four-page textual analysis deploying at least two concepts or ideas we had discussed. Students were asked to select a news article; a relevant, immigration-related website; a TV news segment; a film sequence; or another source and analyze its use of language and/or imagery based on class discussions, lectures, assigned readings, and more. They were required to choose texts they deemed representative of a trend for which they needed to briefly provide a framework of understanding—such background knowledge ought to be rooted on factual information and/or sound research on a given topic. They could also do comparisons between journalistic sources. I provided an example of such media analysis where I compared the coverage of the Syrian refugee "crisis" by two different cable news networks and shows—namely, The O'Reilly Factor on Fox News and The Rachel Maddow Show on MSNBC. I also suggested that a good way to frame the textual analysis was posing a question like, *how do media representations/narratives/discourse of* _____ *contribute to fostering stereotyping of/misconceptions of* _____*?*, and try to answer it by providing a case in point. Overall, students grasped the purpose of the assignment.

Brennan Herring, who describes his experiences below, provided an insightful analysis of materials published on the website of a prominent restrictionist organization, NumbersUSA. In doing so, he identified two widespread trends in conservative media and organizations that exhibit dehumanizing and security-centric language. The paper discussed the framing of immigration in purely numerical terms and argued that doing so is, in itself, dehumanizing because it "completely removes any human element from the discussion." The student also pointed out the repetitive use of words like "aliens" in reference to foreign-born individuals. The paper also showed how NumbersUSA's mission is about "protecting the United States' unique experiment," thus implicitly casting immigrants as a threat to said experiment. The student effectively used cultivation theory to illustrate how this usage promotes negative perceptions of immigrants.

In retrospect, given the starting point of the average honor students that took the class, I believe I/we may have overwhelmed them with too much information—I also provided them with a plethora of research material on Blackboard regarding HB56 and Alabama immigrants, but I doubt most of them even took a look at any of it, given their difficulties with the immediately assigned material. Though I tried to have students connect the dots and take a synoptic look at the issue in its articulation in the media, adding the local aspect as well as attempting to provide basic media literacy skills while teaching a complicated subject like immigration proved to be a challenge. Only truly interested and committed students were able to follow through and obtain actual knowledge. Such successes are illustrated by the testimonies below. Several others struggled to take advantage of having a truly interdisciplinary education on the issue.

LITERATURE UNIT, BY JOHN C. HAVARD

This unit examined three literary works: Anzia Yezierska's "How I Found America," Junot Díaz's *The Brief Wondrous Life of Oscar Wao*, and Lin-Manuel Miranda's *Hamilton*. We spent most of the unit on *Oscar Wao*, discussed at length below. Yezierska's short story is an exploration of immigrants' economic and cultural struggles. I used the story as an entryway into immigrant literature. I used *Hamilton* as a brief look at immigrant culture today, and we examined responses to it to reflect on how polarizing immigration has become (Mele and Healy).

We presented literature as an artistic mode of discourse that reflects on the raw material of history and media that students had studied up to this point. I began the unit by describing Aristotle's description of poetry as a philosophical mode that creatively explores "probability and necessity," that is, how certain types of people are likely to act and what the necessary consequences of their actions are (54). I suggested that although the works we studied might be about fictitious individuals, their characters acted in ways that are probable and necessary for immigrants in their circumstances. As such, the works provide avenues for reflecting on enduring aspects of the immigrant experience. I presented the characters and narratives in the works as abstract reflections on the matters we had previously studied in the history and media units. The literature unit thus served not just as an introduction to immigrant writers but also as a means to reflect back on what we had learned over the course of the semester.

I also explained Aristotle's claim that great tragedy elicits "catharsis" from audiences by provoking "pity and fear" (50). I stressed that a work's success in doing so hinges on whether it engages the audience's capacity for empathy. The audience member will only pity a tragic character if s/he is sufficiently likeable so that the tragedy is not simply just desserts, and the audience will only feel fear if what happened to the character seems like something that could happen to anyone (Aristotle 58–61). (Interestingly, Aristotle's theories are arguably confirmed by neuroscientific research that suggests that reading literary fiction expands our capacity for empathy [Chiaet].) We asked students to consider how the works of literature challenged their capacity for empathy, hoping to engage students' identification with immigrants to achieve our course's diversity and global learning goals.

The unit culminated in an assignment to write a short paper on Díaz's novel. Students were told they could bring in one of the other two assigned works but were required to focus on *Oscar Wao*, which was the unit's centerpiece. The assignment required them to analyze how the novel explores one of the themes we discussed in the history and/or media units. We asked students to identify such a theme, to analyze how the work discusses the theme, and to reflect on what the work says about the theme. I emphasized that effective literary criticism must be rooted in careful reading of concrete passages from a literary work. We thus asked students to examine a few specific such passages as they explored their chosen topic. To challenge students to really focus on the literary text itself, we explicitly forbade use of outside sources.

We spent most of the class time having students practice the mode of analysis the assignment asked them to demonstrate. We began sessions by breaking students into groups to address the three main assignment prompts: (1) Identify one theme that we have discussed this semester that is addressed in the novel, (2) identify at least one specific passage from the day's assigned reading that addresses it, and (3) discuss what the passage reveals about the theme. Each group then reported back to the entire class for further discussion. I kept the discussions on task by reminding students to stay focused on specific passages in the literary works and to keep their interpretations and reflections on the broader themes of immigration rooted in those passages. Moreover, while these sessions mostly comprised student-driven discussion, I regularly intervened with mini-lectures on background information regarding the writers, definitions of literary concepts such as nonlinear narration, and subtleties in the works the students were not picking up on. During one class on *Oscar Wao*, we shared Chimamanda Adichie's TED Talk "The Danger of a Single Story" to spur thinking about how harmful stereotypes can be.

This approach yielded stimulating discussion, particularly about *Oscar Wao*. Most students seemed engrossed by the novel's unique narrative voice and compelling subject matter. Some commented as much on course evaluations. Among the immigration-related themes we discussed in response to prompt one, the two most prominent were probably oppressive dictatorship as a push factor spurring immigration and the psychological damage caused by demeaning stereotypes regarding immigrants. The novel provides a powerful picture of the traumatizing effects of the Trujillo regime on the fictional Cabral family, the effects of which eventually propel Belicia Cabral to the United States. Moreover, stereotypes regarding Dominican masculinity and femininity fuel the novel's conflict. The title character, Oscar, struggles with depression because he is ridiculed for not fitting the stereotype of the attractive, sexually adroit Dominican male. On the other hand, the narrator, Yunior, finds that his success in fitting the same stereotype makes it uncool for him to embrace his love of writing and that it undermines his relationships with the girlfriends he habitually cheats on, especially Oscar's sister Lola. These traumas are spurred by the two characters being subject to a "single story," to use Adichie's term. As a student who had spent time in the Dominican Republic pointed out, these stereotypes are prevalent not only in the Dominican diaspora but in the Dominican Republic itself. However, we linked the theme to immigration by pointing out that the stereotype fueled the rise of the Trujillo regime by enabling him to appeal to a cult of masculinity. Moreover, the novel suggests that immigration exacerbates the stereotype, as Oscar and Yunior find shelter in an idealized conception of their homeland due to their struggles with their families' new home.

We also had many fruitful discussions of our second prompt, *how* the novel explored such concepts. For instance, we discussed how Yunior brings us into contact with the horrors of the Trujillo regime via a nonlinear narrative structure, one instance of which is seen as the novel moves backward over the course of the first few sections of the work: "GhettoNerd at the End of the World" is set from 1974 to 1987 but mostly after 1985, when Oscar is finishing high school and entering college; "Wildwood" is set from 1982 to 1985, as Lola rebels against her mother as a teenager; and "The Three Heartbreaks of Belicia Cabral" is set from 1955 to 1962, as Belicia, Oscar and Lola's mother, struggles through young adulthood and finally immigrates to the United States after she is targeted by the Trujillo family because she has an affair with Trujillo's sister's husband. Although the narrative then returns to the present of Oscar's college and post-college years, Yunior later takes us into the past again for "Poor Abelard," which is set in 1944–1946 and focuses on Belicia's father being imprisoned and tortured for resisting Trujillo's desire to sleep with another one of his daughters.

We finally postulated a variety of conclusions in response to the third prompt, *what* the work was saying about the theme. This prompt asked students to generalize from the work to get to Aristotle's stage of universality. For instance, in discussing push factors and the nonlinear narrative, we hypothesized that the kinds of traumas immigrants experience spur the need for psychological coping mechanisms. In Yunior's case, this is a career as a writer who delves into his community's past as part of a search for origins and explanations for who he is.

The quality of student work on the assignment varied. Some students made interesting observations about passages from the novel but struggled to synthesize them into a compelling conclusion. Some needed work in writing mechanics. Another had apparently not read *Oscar Wao* before writing the paper. I believe their struggles spoke to a couple of factors. First of all, none of these students were English majors, and only a couple were liberal arts majors. None had taken any literature coursework past sophomore surveys in British, American, or World literature, and some had yet to take those courses. Thus, while students in general were stimulated by *Oscar Wao*, they generally lacked sufficient experience writing about literature to write effective papers, even with the practice we provided in class. This challenge speaks to a related complication in teaching this interdisciplinary class: We packed three disciplinary units into this semester-long course while also asking students to write a research paper. The combination of cognitive overload as we moved between these units, along with the lack of sufficient time devoted to any one of them, likely worked against students' mastery. They needed more time with literature to do what I was asking them to do effectively.

However, some students got the idea and wrote strong essays. For instance, one wrote on Díaz's use of the Spanish language as well as lingo regarding science fiction, fantasy, and comic books drawn from nerd culture. One of the work's most striking features is that its narration is liberally sprinkled with Spanish and nerd language; much of the Spanish is Dominican slang and most of it is unitalicized and unglossed. This aspect is noted by virtually all readers and has been the focus of a great deal of scholarly analysis (e.g., Norman). The student argued that the challenge that non-Spanish speakers experience while reading the work places them in the shoes of immigrants, who are similarly forced to navigate a new language and culture. Although the paper had organizational and mechanical problems, it effectively engaged the three aspects of the assignment. First of all, in touching on Díaz's commentary on immigration and assimilation, it identified a theme the novel addressed that we had discussed throughout the semester. As the student wrote, the reader's experience resembles the challenge of immigration: "Similar to immigrants arriving and adjusting to foreign lands, the inability to read, let alone understand, the new language can create obstacles capable of drastic setbacks, involving work, housing, or health. They are forced to use context clues, hand motions, and translators, that take up so much time, to be merely understood, yet never fully satisfied." Second of all, it addressed how the novel went about doing so by identifying relevant formal characteristics in the novel's narrative voice, the use of Spanish and nerd language. As the student continued from the quote above,

> I could never fully comprehend the spanish, let alone the nerd lingo that consisted of words like "Sycorax" (84 Diaz) or "Mordar" (78 Diaz), when relating to some evil villain and his lair. Diaz rarely, if ever, stopped or slowed to explain what I perceived as gibberish actually was, leaving me confused and out of tune with those more fluent in such languages, hitting the head on the nail when it comes to immigrants.

Finally, the student explored what the novel reveals about immigration: In placing the reader in the role of the immigrant, it expands the reader's capacity for empathy with the immigrant experience. As the student wrote, "The greatest relation between immigrants and this novel is the hopeful expectations that the characters have for a better future and the mental/physical trauma caused by a possible threat to that future." The cognitive dissonance the novel inspires in readers gives them an inkling, however small, of the traumas of being an immigrant, a valuable experience in a culture in which such empathy is sorely lacking. The student arrived at this conclusion by reflecting on the novel's commentary on matters such as assimilation that we had discussed throughout the semester, thus satisfying the basic goal of the assignment.

STUDENT SUCCESS STORIES

Brennan Herring's Experience

The immigration seminar showed me that there is much more to immigration than I previously understood. Growing up in a conservative household, the opinions and perspectives I have been exposed to are fairly one-dimensional. While not all of the opinions I held before I took the class changed, it showed me that immigration is an issue with a great amount of complexity that requires more examination than many political pundits give it. One of the most compelling illustrations of this came from the personal stories we heard from many immigrants affected by recent changes in immigration policies in Alabama. Exposure to the circumstances that brought them into their current situation made me more conscious of immigration's human element, which is often lost when talking about the legal and economic aspects of the issue.

Because immigration is such a contentious issue, I learned that it can be difficult to know whether the sources of the information we have are operating from an honest point of view. Many resources on immigration tend to only focus on one aspect of the issue and misrepresent other parts of it. These sources paint an inaccurate picture of the lives of immigrants and the issues important to them. When I started to examine what it means to be an immigrant in today's culture, I began to understand how important it is to critically evaluate the sources I had for information regarding immigration.

Through the lessons I learned in the immigration seminar, I gained insight into the lives of immigrants that are subject to the perceptions and laws concerning immigrants in the United States. In today's political climate, immigration has become a very emotionally charged issue, with many blaming immigrants for social and economic problems and pursuing policies that would inhibit their ability to live peacefully and comfortably in the United States. I was exposed to the real struggles that immigrants face in light of the direction of immigration policy in many states. Especially here in Alabama with the passing of HB 56 and the uncertainty surrounding the future of DACA recipients, immigrants are caught in a web of doubt and volatility that makes them unsure of where their future might be headed. As I took this class, I realized that the continuing education of multiple students I knew would be endangered if DACA were repealed.

In a more holistic sense, the seminar made me think about how immigrants should be treated in a just society. What should the nature of immigration restrictions be? At what point do immigration restrictions start to become oppressive and counterproductive to the economic and societal health of the United States? More than the answers that I learned from the class, the questions that it left me thinking about have made me question preconceived notions about how immigration should be treated in the United States and how perceptions of immigrants are unjustly affecting the lives of those that have come to the United States in search for a better life.

Rachel Pate's Experience

This course expanded my knowledge and understanding both of the topic and of the importance of immigration. Because we were presented with three methods of viewing immigration, I came to a much greater appreciation of the topic's complexity. Within the methods, I was able to analyze contrasting views and stances to see that the differences and issues have roots much farther back in our nation's history than I previously realized. In conjunction with my studies on the history of Latin America, I began to learn more about reasons for immigration to the United States and the history of how those immigrants have been treated—for better or worse. The historical component helped me recognize the complexity of immigration. The various motivations people have for immigrating are more often than not products of history, and the historical analysis of the origins of the immigration debate benefited my understanding of today's conflict.

In terms of that conflict, the media portion of the class opened my eyes to the nature of media. Though aware that I shouldn't believe everything I read on the internet, it is difficult to evaluate what I should and should not believe. To intentionally analyze media articles for their slant and bias made it much easier to recognize in day-to-day reading on current events. Being taught to recognize and interpret the bias of media is much more practical than being taught that media has bias, so the weekly experience of documenting and summarizing current event articles proved very useful to me as a student and a citizen. Awareness of valid sources and verifiable information is key, and the best way for me to learn that was through the experience of picking out what is and is not good information in an article. In addition, the media portion of the class helped me more clearly form and understand my own opinions and stances on immigration, especially regarding how I can better articulate those views to others.

This formulation and articulation are fueled most strongly, though, by the stories behind the people who immigrate. The literature section of the course strongly impacted my ideas about people who immigrate and immigration as a whole. *The Brief Wondrous Life of Oscar Wao* gave me a much greater respect for the people throughout history who have left their homes by choice or were forced to forge a new life. The emotional aspect of storytelling is vital to the subject of immigration, because it is what humanizes the subject. Interviewing a close friend of mine was without a doubt the most impactful assignment of the course. When my friend chose to speak up as a Dreamer and allow me to interview her, I had to reevaluate my own stances on immigration. Immigration can be a faceless abstraction but putting human faces or names to the subject makes it that much more urgent to find a way to help.

When I realized that my views—and therefore my votes—affect people that I know and love, it changed the discussion for me. Putting into words the experiences of my friend was a whole new experience that was outside my comfort zone, but without the process of interviewing my friend I would have remained unaware of an issue that is now very important to me. The interview piqued my interest in traumas experienced by children who migrate or are the children of people who migrate and how that affects their lives and health. Children experiencing preventable trauma is an injustice I feel strongly that we as individuals must work harder to prevent, and immigration itself is traumatic enough without its companion issues of racism/nationalism and language acquisition. The research paper process helped me to learn and explore the topic, but ultimately the paper, the interview, and the class as a whole taught me that I need to help others to be more aware of the issues in our society and how they are affecting our neighbors, friends, coworkers, loved ones, and acquaintances. Immigration does not just affect those who migrate, and the complexity of the issue necessitates that more than just those who migrate must be aware. In the end, it is a human issue, one that can only be solved by cooperation and genuine concern for the wellbeing of even the most distant of other people.

CONCLUSION

These students' experiences illustrate some of the successes we had. Many students gained a deeper understanding of the immigrant experience through writing and research. As noted, though, the course was not without its challenges, and we conclude by discussing two notable ones. First of all, we simultaneously came to feel the course was overly ambitious and overwhelming to students, even while fretting that we were not covering essential aspects of the topic. A case in point was our current events scrapbook. We came up with the idea to include this assignment only a few weeks before the beginning of the semester, when it dawned upon us that requiring students to complete a formal assignment to keep up with the evolution of current events related to immigration would provide ready opportunities for us to discuss the latest news on the topic. At this point, we had already planned the history, media, and literature units. The assignment did provide a crucial learning experience; students were generally unaware of current events related to immigration, and the assignment helped them learn about the issues and understand their importance. However, although many students did their part by diligently keeping up with the assignment throughout the term, we never had the class time to really develop the kinds of conversations about the material that we had hoped to have. Our mistake was likely that we tacked the scrapbook assignment onto our existing course structure rather than planning more carefully and clearing more time for it. We asked students to submit this assignment five times over the course of the semester, and we were only able to devote twenty minutes or so of class time here and there to having students share the current events they were reading and writing about. We could have easily devoted entire class meetings to these discussions and doing so would have likely motivated greater student engagement in reflecting and writing about current developments. However, it would have meant less time to discuss other material we had planned, but it might have been worth it because it would have helped students make connections between the history, media, and literature units and current events. Such connections would have reinforced the global citizenship and diversity outcomes for our course by spurring greater recognition of the relationship between the academic units and the equity issues students are seeing in the daily news cycle.

A second challenge pertained to encouraging students to choose research projects related to their majors and career aspirations. Some students found more success in this endeavor than others. A student studying Communication Disorders, as stated, devised a project touching on the benefits of bilingual education programs for immigrant students with communication troubles. Another student who aspires to attend medical school wrote a very effective research paper about the impact the Trump administration's travel ban against majority-Muslim nations might have on the influx of needed immigrant physicians from these countries. However, others struggled. An aspiring nurse had a good idea to research the push-pull factors leading nurses to immigrate to the United States, but the research did not yield much meaningful information or an effective paper. We encouraged a computer science major to research the effects of brain drain in STEM fields on home countries from which talented professionals immigrate, but the student struggled to establish traction on the topic and switched to another one that failed to maintain her interest and that did not lead to an impressive paper. We concluded that these students could have used more one-on-one counseling in the research process. We did meet with each student, but perhaps we could have scheduled for more such meetings by cancelling class time; however, the ambitious agenda for the course made it difficult to devote more one-on-one time with students. Moreover, our own disciplinary backgrounds in liberal arts left us poorly equipped to help students with research techniques in STEM fields. Students may have benefited if we had recruited assistance from other faculty who were more familiar with the types of research done in these fields. If given the chance to teach the course again, we would keep such challenges in mind.

WORKS CITED

"About El Refugio." *El Refugio,* https://www.elrefugiostewart.org/about-us/. Accessed 19 March 2018.

Adichie, Chimamanda. "The Danger of a Single Story." *TED,* July 2009, https://www.ted.com/talks/chimamanda_ngozi_adichie_the_danger_of_a_single_story?language=en.

Aristotle. *Poetics.* Translated by James Hutton, Norton, 1982.

Buchanan, Patrick. "Will the West Survive the Century?" *Creators,* 5 Jul. 2016, https://www.creators.com/read/pat-buchanan/07/16/will-the-west-survive-the-century.

Chavez, Leo R. *The Latino Threat Narrative: Constructing Immigrants, Citizens, and the Nation,* 2nd ed. Stanford University Press, 2013.

Chiaet, Julianne. "Novel Finding: Reading Literary Fiction Improves Empathy." *Scientific American,* 4 Oct. 2013, https://www.scientificamerican.com/article/novel-finding-reading-literary-fiction-improves-empathy/.

Chomsky, Aviva. *Undocumented: How Immigration Became Illegal.* Beacon Press, 2014.

Colford, Paul. "'Illegal Immigrant' No More." *AP Definitive Source,* 2 Apr. 2013, https://blog.ap.org/announcements/illegal-immigrant-no-more.

Gerber, David. *American Immigration: A Very Short Introduction.* Oxford UP, 2011.

Giagnoni, Silvia. *Here We May Rest: Alabama Immigrants in the Age of HB56.* NewSouth Books, 2017.

Hall, Stuart. "Encoding and Decoding in the Television Discourse." *Culture, Media, Language: Working Papers in Cultural Studies, 1972–79,* edited by Stuart Hall et al., Routledge, 1991, pp. 117–127.

Havard, John C. *Hispanicism and Early US Literature: Spain, Mexico, Cuba, and the Origins of US National Identity.* University of Alabama Press, 2018.

Henderson, Timothy J. *Beyond Borders: A History of Mexican Migration to the United States.* Wiley-Blackwell, 2011.

"Honors Courses." *Auburn University at Montgomery,* https://www.aum.edu/courses/. Accessed 26 Feb. 2018.

"CNN's Jim Acosta Goes Head to Head with Stephen Miller." *YouTube,* uploaded by *Los Angeles Times,* 2 Aug. 2017, https://www.youtube.com/watch?v=kSJ-gS7lmyw.

Mele, Christopher, and Patrick Healy. "*Hamilton* Had Some Unscripted Lines for Pence. Trump Wasn't Happy." *The New York Times*, 19 Nov. 2016, https://www.nytimes.com /2016/11/19/us/mike-pencehamilton.html.

Negrón-Muntaner, Frances, et al. *The Latino Media Gap: A Report on the State of Latinos in U.S. Media.* Center for the Study of Ethnicity and Race, June 2014, https://www .latinorebels.com/2014/06/17/the-latino-media-gap-a-report-on-the-state-of-latinos-in -u-s-media/.

Norman, Rachel. "'A Bastard Jargon': Language Politics and Identity in *The Brief Wondrous Life of Oscar Wao.*" *South Atlantic Review*, vol. 81, no. 1, 2016, pp. 34–50.

Picker, Miguel, and Chyng Sun. *Latinos Beyond Reel: Challenging a Media Stereotype.* Media Education Foundation, 2012.

Santa Ana, Otto. "The Cowboy and the Goddess: Television News Mythmaking about Immigrants." *Discourse & Society*, vol. 27, no. 1, 2015, pp. 95–117.

Thompson, Christie. "Welcome to Stewart Detention Center, the Black Hole of America's Immigration System." *Vice*, 11 Dec. 2016, https://www.vice.com/en/article/ypv59j /welcome-to-stewart-detention-center-the-black-hole-of-the-immigration-system.

Tobar, Héctor. "Avoiding the Trap of Immigration Porn." *The New York Times*, 7 Aug. 2018, https://www.nytimes.com/2017/08/07/opinion/immigration-porn-photography -deportation.html.

"UHP Outcome Rubric." PDF file. Accessed at Auburn University at Montgomery, 26 Feb. 2018.

Vargas, José Antonio. "My Life as an Undocumented Immigrant." *The New York Times*, 22 Jun. 2011, https://www.nytimes.com/2011/06/26/magazine/my-life-as-an-undocu mented-immigrant.html.

Yezierska, Anzia. *How I Found America: Collected Stories of Anzia Yezierska.* Persea, 1991.

Zinn, Howard. *The Southern Mystique.* 1967. Haymarket Books, 2013.

Zong, Jie, and Jeanne Batalova. "Frequently Requested Statistics on Immigrants and Immigration in the United States." *Migration Policy Institute*, 8 Mar. 2017, https://www .migrationpolicy.org/article/frequently-requested-statistics-immigrants-and-immigra tion-united-states-2020.

9

REFLECTIVE PRACTICE, IMMIGRANT NARRATIVES, AND THE HUMANITIES INSTITUTE

Heather Ostman

In 2012, several colleagues and I established the Humanities Institute at the New York suburban community college where I teach—the result of a generous National Endowment for the Humanities grant and the further generosity of local donors, but also the result of intentional pedagogical practice, specifically practice that engages student reflection and immigrant narratives that emerged in several composition courses on campus. I have been the director of the Humanities Institute since 2013, and the early pedagogical lessons I learned through student reflection—on their writing, on their learning processes, and on the rhetorical strategies they employed in their writing—continue to inform the work of the Humanities Institute, which features the immigrant experience as the central focus of its programming. The primary purpose of the institute has been to foster a deeper understanding across the college and the community of the immigrant experience as expressed within humanities. We[1] have defined "immigrant experience" broadly, an umbrella term that included foreign-born residents, first- and second-generation immigrants, diaspora, voluntary and involuntary immigrants, and more. The idea for the immigration focus, though, stemmed from my own students' writing in my English 101: Research and Writing courses, founded on the premise of Bruno Latour's actor-network theory and engaged reflective practice. My intention for my courses is to enable students to participate in a mindful approach to knowledge production that provided a scaffolding to curricular change and resulted in the establishment of the Humanities Institute at the college. Consequently, the institute further supports reflective practice

---

1.   I will use the pronoun "we" frequently in this paper as acknowledgment of the team that helped to write the grant with us and that continues to support the Humanities Institute's work.

https://doi.org/10.7330/9781646421664.c009

and the articulation of prior learning experiences, particularly for writing students, by prioritizing subordinated and situated knowledges as a means to accessing and engaging academic discourse.

REFLECTIVE PRACTICE AND PRIOR LEARNING EXPERIENCE

As a precursor to the development of the Humanities Institute, previous experience teaching working adults helped me to see more clearly the relationships between prior learning (knowledge produced before enrolling in academia or between institutions) and learning in the college setting. As an English professor, my interest in these relationships has primarily focused on the ways students articulate their knowledge, particularly in a setting that sets certain—if sometimes ambiguous—parameters around what kinds of knowledge are considered "legitimate." Narrative practice is one method used in higher education to facilitate prior learning assessment (PLA), especially knowledge acquired outside of the general university curriculum and therefore often viewed through the traditional/conventional academic lens as less valid. This is a tacit designation that can include subordinated knowledge, situated knowledge, and other forms of learning that occur in nonlinear ways and/or in nontraditional settings. Other common forms of PLA can include standardized tests such as CLEP and others, but in certain instances essays provide a viable way for students to legitimize their earlier learning by qualifying and quantifying it through academic discourse and ultimately the award of college credit. It is through narrative practice and composition that I gained my appreciation for PLA and its ability to facilitate the articulation of knowledge production.

My colleague Cathy Leaker and I have studied the intersections of PLA practice and composition, particularly insofar as PLA essays drew frequently from narrative and other common rhetorical practices as a way to articulate and thus "qualify" nontraditional spaces for learning and the knowledge produced in these spaces. Cathy and I found through multi-year studies that PLA practice had much to offer composition studies because the essays our students were writing not only employed multiple rhetorical strategies (compare/contrast, definition, division/classification, narrative, and others) but necessarily enacted reflective practice. Through our students' essays, we began to see a parallel with Kathleen Yancey's claim that "Reflection asks that we explain to others . . . so that in explaining to others, we explain to ourselves. We begin to re-understand" (24). Although we were interested in our students' prior learning, our interest—and my primary interest still—was how that learning could be articulated and how the writing itself could be instrumental in further learning. For Yancey, the intentional act of introspection provides a space for reflective practice; however, she additionally underscores the value in "reflective re-understanding" as students articulate their knowledge in writing for an imagined audience; they gain a deeper understanding, what she terms "reflection-in-presentation" (13). Cathy and I extended Yancey's notion of "reflection-in-presentation" to our work with students' PLA essays, along with the assumption that "the PLA essay process as a reflective exercise should do more than transform and deepen the learning that began before the student arrived at the university, but should extend that learning to the act of its own articulation" (Leaker and Ostman 697–698). In other words, writing and reflection were essential elements in the process of continuous learning *through writing*.

My experience with narrative PLA practice has provided the foundation for reflective practice and has become a central guide in my approach with my English 101: Writing and Research courses in my current teaching setting at a community college. English 101 at my institution is the first-year, credit-bearing composition course, which has an emphasis on research and documentation. My earlier work with adult and other nontraditional learners codified for me the essential role prior learning of all kinds plays in the process of knowledge production. Further, acknowledging and drawing on students' prior learning enables them to negotiate the claimed authority of institutional knowledge and articulate the myriad knowledges they bring to the college and develop once there. Reflective practice, then, is essential, especially since it offers students an opportunity to recognize, re-understand, reaffirm, and extend the knowledge they have. This is an essential element because, while many community college students have had satisfactory educational experiences, often we, their instructors, also see students who are disenfranchised learners, coming from challenging educational experiences in the past and consequently exhibiting uncertainty over the value of the knowledge they bring to the institution. Furthermore, as many of our immigrant students have come from various educational backgrounds, privileging prior learning experiences and engaging reflective practice has enabled many students to articulate their knowledge both before coming to college and during their enrollment now that they are here. Therefore, emphasizing that knowledge produced in an academic setting is as essential as knowledge produced in nonacademic settings has been crucial to learning to access and engage academic discourse to articulate students' myriad ways of knowing.

There is a wide breadth of scholarship on the legitimacy and importance of nontraditional ways of knowing to support our work with
these students. Tara Fenwick and Richard Edwards cite multiple studies
ranging from feminist studies of knowledge production (notably Linda
Alcoff and Elizabeth Potter's work) to scientific and technological studies of knowledge production (a prolific range of work by Bruno Latour,
including his early work with Steve Woolgar) to sociologies of knowledge
production (see Karin Knorr Cetina) and to indigenous knowledge
production (notably the collective studies edited in *Indigenous Knowledge*
edited by Malia Villegas et al.). Fenwick and Edwards note that all of
these studies and more "have shown that scholarship practices of making or using knowledge cannot be separated from everyday practices
and experiences of knowledge generation" (37). Similarly, education
scholar Mike Rose has studied the richness and depth of situated and
contextualized knowledges, particularly within the context of the workplace; he argues for the recognition of the parallel processes of knowledge production within this context as a legitimate and authoritative site
of knowledge production. For example, he points to studies of factory
workers who become skilled and "learn to work smart, to maximize
energy and efficiency," and further:

> Moving from the factory to the other "old economy" manual work, the
> picture gets more textured. Mechanics, machinists, and all the construc-
> tion tradespersons continually blend hand and brain. They develop rich
> knowledge of materials, tools, and processes. They regularly troubleshoot
> and solve problems. And each trade affords the opportunity to learn
> and keep learning and to develop competencies. Take, for example, the
> carpenter who uses a number of mathematical concepts—symmetry, pro-
> portion, congruence, the properties of angles—and develops the ability
> to visualize these concepts while building a cabinet, a flight of stairs, a
> pitched roof. (78–79)

Importantly, embedded within the carpenter's situated knowledge are
principle concepts that are also found in college-level mathematics
curricula. One objective of PLA—and this is a bit of a side note—is to
identify the parallels in nontraditional sites of knowledge production
and their results; another objective, of course, is to validate other nontraditional sites that do not share parallels to a college curriculum but
that nonetheless produce valuable, legitimate knowledges. Still, Rose's
example of the carpenter's work is similar to countless other workplace
contexts where learning processes—drawing information from multiple
sources and synthesizing information and knowledge to produce further
knowledge—is duplicated.

For the purposes here, it is important that Rose appears to support Fenwick and Edwards's validation of Latour's framework for viewing knowledge through the lens of network relationships, known as actor-network theory (ANT). This theory foregrounds the context of relationships in knowledge production as essential to estimating the value of the knowledge—in other words, as essential to determining the authority of knowledge. Actor-network theory is essential in qualifying nonacademic knowledge that does not demonstrate parallels to a college curriculum's learning objectives. Through this lens, as Fenwick and Edwards argue, knowledge production is an effect:

> The point is that knowledge, as well as subjects, objects, and systems, is taken to be an *effect* of connections and activity, performed into existence in webs of relations. There are no received categories. Disciplinary canons then are not simply received; their reception requires certain practices, discourses, inscriptions and rituals. . . . As Latour (2005) has long argued, we tend not to see the networks that are continually assembling and reassembling to bring forth and sustain what we authorize as knowledge. (38–39)

Fenwick and Edwards' 2014 study asserts the multiple forces that engage to produce knowledge and concludes that "knowledge cannot be viewed as coherent, transcendent, generalisable, unproblematic or inherently powerful. . . . The thing is not separate from the knowing that gathers and authorises it as a thing" (47). They see knowledge production and the validation of knowledge as the result of certain subjective processes and relationships. Therefore:

> Knowledge is revealed to be, not a body or an authority, but an effect of connections performed into existence in webs of relations that are worked at, around and against constantly. These are always precarious because they are filled with ongoing controversy, "matters of concern," despite the press to resolve and black box these. . . . Network approaches trace the process through which diverse elements become combined into knowledge networks, and how some networks stabilise, extend, enroll others and circulate to exert power, while others dissolve, distort, mutate or become appropriated. (48)

For my students, the recognition of actor-network relationships has direct consequences because it makes space in the academy for the acknowledgment and use of nonlinear and nontraditional ways of knowing.

Fenwick and Edwards conclude their study by claiming that network approaches to knowledge production have implications for curriculum development. Their study maps ways of enabling students to trace the networks at work during processes of knowing, a direction beyond the scope of this essay, but the inherent principle of reflection and articulation in their work offer a context for discussing my own students and their work in English 101. While Fenwick and Edwards' study does not delineate the various directions those developments may go, their study illuminates the direction of my own courses, as my students are asked to draw on prior learning and contextualized learning as they develop their research paper topics. This approach has been effective particularly among many foreign-born students, and it has since become a central component in the Humanities Institute's offerings. The institution where I teach is a mid-sized community college located in the suburbs of New York City, where one in four residents is foreign-born. The college is a designated Hispanic-Serving Institution (HSI), but many students hail from nations on four continents, as well as native-born students with multiple generations born within the United States but originating elsewhere. The rich ethnic and international backgrounds and experiences students bring with them to the classroom inform their educational experiences, naturally, and their own individual ways of knowing. And while it is also beyond the scope of this essay to measure exactly how their backgrounds and experiences contribute to the networks of their knowing, the theoretical work provided by Fenwick and Edwards, as well as the foundational work by Latour, provide space for the assumption that these various backgrounds necessarily offer an opportunity for students to draw from the knowing they have developed on their way to the classroom.

THE COMPOSITION CLASSROOM AND THE IMMIGRANT EXPERIENCE

To engage students' experiential and situated knowledges, English 101 presumes that students are entitled to own and direct their continued knowledge production. Loosely based on Adam Fletcher's 2005 study, *Meaningful Student Involvement Guide to Students as Partners in School Change*, the course engages Pauline Billett and Dona Martin's five principle ideas:

1. Involvement with textbooks and other reading materials
2. Connecting curriculum to life goals
3. Students aiding in the teaching process
4. Students as professional-development partners
5. Students as decision makers

Like Fletcher, Billett and Martin acknowledge—and perhaps emphasize the obvious point—that "students who actively engage during class are less bored, find the learning process more rewarding and engage in deeper learning." I certainly agree. Therefore, before the Humanities Institute was even conceived as an idea, my students' research projects developed from their own interests and knowledge. As a preliminary step, then as now, when my students are developing research questions, they are asked to develop a library of their collective textual recommendations that correspond with their chosen topics. They are encouraged to work in research groups when there are commonalities among their interests, so they may develop a shared collection of resources.

But in 2011, two things occurred: several students kept recommending books about immigration and others were writing narratives about their refugee and immigration experiences. The combination of these two events caused me to pay attention to what my students were telling me: that their migrations—in the myriad ways they found their way to my classroom, to New York State, to the United States—had influenced how they viewed their education, where they saw themselves going from here, and consequently how they understood what they had come to know.

One student in particular recommended *First Crossings: Stories about Teen Immigrants*, edited by Donald R. Gallo (Candlewick Press, 2004, 2007). She was adamant about the relevance of this book to all of my students, because she believed it enabled them to find their writing voices and by extension, their research topics. Research project topics have varied in my courses over the years, but that year students were asked to pose a research question and shape their topics from there. This particular student and a few of her peers began to pose research questions about immigration, a topic they had each experienced at different times in their lives. They sought to research causes, challenges, and outcomes of immigration, many of which were situated in their first-hand experiences. Their relationships to the subject matter as well as to each other enacted Latour's actor-network theory, thereby building "legitimacy" around the knowledges stemming from their immigrant experiences. *First Crossings* therefore became part of their collective library, since the text presents a series of teenagers' stories about migration and their experiences in the new places they found themselves in. Inherent in all of the stories is a network of knowing and articulation of that knowledge. When this student presented the book to her research group, it seemed particularly relevant to their studies. The stories follow a linear model, but all provide knowledge—in English, intended for imagined audiences of teens and their educators. The stories replicate a learning model that mostly narrates the process of knowing in a linear form—a

form well known to my students, but situates the learning in the context
of immigration, following the formulaic structure of what the narrators
of each story know and tracing through time how they came to know
what they know now. My students engaged Fletcher's additional four
principle ideas and developed projects that drew from prior knowledge
of emigration/immigration, America as a new home, and what conditions were like in America. They directed their research toward their
life goals, allowing their intentions—usually educational goals such as
transfer or training for a job—to figure into how deeply they explored
their topics. Through presentation and small group work students educated each other and created a broader, classroom-based actor-network
of knowledge.

Because of the rich research many of these students produced and
because of their investment in the topics they developed, Fletcher's
model provided a basis for the subject matter and for the development
of reflective practice both in my later English 101 courses and then soon
after in a significant area of the humanities curriculum at the college. I
used the broad topic of immigration for a subsequent research project
in a following semester—this was a departure from the more open-
ended topics I have previously assigned. Students drew from books and
materials they had discovered and contributed to a repository of information for all. Then drawing from Yancey's portfolio work, we used her
template of contexts for reflection and understanding knowledge production. Students were given the tools for extending the multiplicity of
knowledges they brought to the classroom—experiential, situated, and
academic—and for creating platforms for further knowledge production. A model that also proved effective from my earlier PLA narrative
essay practice, Yancey's contextual practices provided the scaffolding
for students to build knowledge during the composing/writing of their
research essays, while drawing on their own immigrant stories (or less
frequently, those they read about).

Yancey proposes multiple contexts within her discussion of portfolios
for articulating knowledge; each context relies on a distinct set of rhetorical strategies for the expression of knowledge. I found her engagement
of multiple contexts as spaces for considering and articulating knowing
to be very useful in facilitating the reflective processes during the assessment of prior learning (in my earlier work) and later in the context
of my students' research projects on the/an immigrant experience.
In her study, "Postmodernism, Palimpsest, and Portfolios: Theoretical
Issues in the Representation of Student Work" (2004), Yancey delineates several contexts that enable students to articulate their learning:

temporal, spatial, and political. The first of these, the temporal context, is reflected in many of the linear stories found in the Gallo volume; they trace what students knew at an earlier point and how that led to what they know now (Yancey 741). The narrative, linear model is obviously a familiar rhetorical approach for students, and while the articulation of knowledge in the linear model can be engaging, it does not prepare students necessarily for college-level study and the employment of academic discourse. However, as an introductory text to immigrant stories and knowledge production, it offers access for many students.

To also enable students to perform college-level work, two other contexts that Yancey identifies became essential: the spatial context, which enables students to make comparisons and contrasts to other spaces where knowledge production occurs for them, and the sociopolitical context, which enables students to express/address their awareness of their audiences. Through instructor guidance, when students were able to reflect on how they learned and where they were also learning or had learned something related to their topics (i.e., in their own migrations, in their contact with American culture, in their relating to their peers, in their learning in other classrooms, etc.), they began to trace their own networks of knowledge production. This self-conscious shift in reflection, in knowing how they know and comparing knowledge to other situations and types of knowledges, later provided the necessary scaffolding for reworking a significant aspect of the humanities curriculum.

THE HUMANITIES INSTITUTE

The Humanities Institute at the college was conceived as a way to develop and redirect the humanities curriculum through enriching classroom practice and programming. My students' research essays about immigrant topics, which intentionally included reflection on ways of knowing, inspired our National Endowment for the Humanities (NEH) Community College Challenge Grant application to found the college's Humanities Institute. When my colleagues and I first started to think about the possibilities for the NEH grant, we knew that Eurocentered narratives and beliefs about teaching and about the college's students were still dominating curricular development, even though the college and its foundation had funded the development of a community center/building dedicated to meeting immigrant needs in the surrounding community. While that center was viewed as a community-based program, it was also viewed as separate and not an academic initiative. And despite the fact of the college's

Hispanic-Serving Institution (HSI) status and New York location, it appeared that the academic side of the college had not considered the demographics of its students as its humanities curriculum developed over the years. Therefore, given my own students' self-directed research and interests, an institute with funding committed to foregrounding the immigrant experience seemed to be a logical extension of a curricular-level effort.

As the Humanities Institute's director, I have come to see how creating significant cultural change in a college stems from a systemic refocusing, reprioritizing—which began in my own English classrooms and extended into a re-visioning of the humanities curriculum. And how timely this change has been: Immigration is now at the forefront of urgent national and political dialogues (and arguments) across the United States. Seven years ago, we never imagined the direction these dialogues would take—spanning from the federal threat to (and now actual) end the Deferred Action for Childhood Arrivals (DACA) program, the separation of immigrant children from their undocumented parents (Davis), a redefining of asylum criteria (Lynch and Levinson), and more. But in retrospect, as an educator, I realize how well-positioned the Humanities Institute is to help inform these and other college conversations and classrooms that try to address immigration-related topics in the United States today. Through the collective efforts of many individuals at the college, the Humanities Institute has become a viable and vibrant initiative, one that supports and enriches the humanities curriculum through a variety of programming at the institution and helps to keep the experience of the immigrant at the center of many college-wide dialogues.

The Humanities Institute offers a model for creating a space for immigrant narratives both at the classroom level and at the institutional level, and its curricular enrichment activities support prior learning experiences and foster reflective practice in the writing workshops offered each semester. Because of the links between prior learning and the immigrant experience, the Humanities Institute enables the college to now offer a dedicated space for pedagogies that incorporate immigrant narratives. The mission of the Humanities Institute projected our early, bold hopes; when my colleagues and I first designed it, the mission was more of a projection than a reality:

> The Westchester Community College Humanities Institute is a natural and logical extension of the College's intellectual commitment to immigrant education. The humanities include many forms of artistic expression, intellectual inquiry, and ordinary life through which people explore

the meanings and challenges of human experience. Moreover, they offer a framework for current debates about nationality, individuality, citizenship, borders, inclusivity, social justice, and cultural identity.

The college's "intellectual commitment to immigrant education" was designated mostly within the confines of the earlier mentioned community center at the college aptly known as "The Gateway Center," where new arrivals to the United States, to the county in particular, could receive assistance with language acquisition, citizenship applications, job searches, and of course, academic bridges to college-level, credit-bearing courses—the Gateway Center only offered non-credit English as a Second Language courses. But we were optimistic as we asserted our hope: that the college would have an intellectual commitment to immigrant education, and therefore, it could support a humanities initiative framed within this commitment.

The Humanities Institute's first year drew on multiple external and internal resources, which had the effect of attracting interest both within and outside the college. Programming over the last seven years has not varied dramatically in terms of the kinds of events the Humanities Institute offers. Events drew from a range of scholars, some locally based—as in, they taught at the college or in the New York City metropolitan area—and some more distantly based. We have drawn presenters from as far as California and even farther internationally, from Qatar and Japan. Although each year's events have a broad theme, programming must support in-class coursework and/ or community-based interests. The events typically include lectures, film screenings, open discussions, and workshops. And all of the events were anchored by a series of workshops and lectures offered by the institute's writer-in-residence, a renowned author contracted for three-year terms. Additionally, the Humanities Institute offers a faculty fellows program that invites colleagues from the college to propose research projects to be funded by the institute with the intention of furthering the immigrant-themed approach to the humanities; priority is also given to proposals that engage a reflective element in their development and assessment.

One of the initial goals of the institute was to enrich the humanities curriculum, and we see evidence of a profound shift away from Eurocentric courses. The narratives of immigrants' experiences permeate all institute programming and manifest in faculty research projects, which translate often into more diverse course material that features the immigrant voice with greater frequency. For instance, English 201, American Literature Since 1865, a course that has been on the books for decades, had traditionally featured predominantly white male authors, such as Whitman, Fitzgerald, Hemingway, and Delillo. In the last several semesters when the course was offered, the syllabus brought texts such as Junot Díaz's *Drown* and Jhumpa Lahiri's *The Namesake*, among other texts that foreground the immigrant experience in the United States. To move the college's humanities offerings toward a curriculum that made space for immigrant voices and narratives, the institute relied on focused program planning, strategic outreach, and consistent communication—resulting from the efforts of numerous college members, but above all draw from the willingness of our students to share their insights, knowledge, and wisdom as we build a more meaningful and reflective curriculum. Therefore, the pedagogical practices that were engaged in English 101—through reflective practice and agent-network theory—have formed the foundation of the Humanities Institute.

As an extension of the earlier work that began with students and prior learning, the institute privileges students' prior knowledge and experiential learning as it fosters further knowledge production within writing classrooms. For instance, in selected writing courses (volunteered by instructors), the Humanities Institute provides a space for reflective practice through writing workshops that are geared toward supporting and enriching writing students. In these workshops, students are invited to participate in writing exercises that enable them to articulate prior learning experiences within their current and comparative learning contexts, employing Yancey's contexts for writing and reflection. The institute offers regularly scheduled workshops for instructors who wish to bring their entire classes to support these intentional levels of reflective practice. We see—anecdotally for now—that students find their prior learning experiences are legitimatized through these kinds of writing exercises, which appear to both support students' confidence in their participation in classes as well as recognize the importance of their prior learning, particularly as it may have occurred in native countries other than the United States. All of this is good, it seems, not only for pedagogical purposes, but for creating safe learning spaces within a political context that at times appears inhospitable at best toward immigrant students.

WORKS CITED

Alcoff, Linda, and Elizabeth Potter, editors. *Feminist Epistemologies*. Routledge, 1992.

Davis, Julie Hirschfeld. "Separated at the Border from Their Parents: In Six Weeks, 1,995 Children." *New York Times*, 15 Jun. 2018, https://www.nytimes.com/2018/06/15/us /politics/trump-immigration-separation-border.html.

Fenwick, Tara, and Richard Edwards. "Networks of Knowledge, Matters of Learning, and Criticality in Higher Education." *Higher Education*, vol. 67, 2014, pp. 35–50.

Latour, Bruno, and Steve Woolgar. *Laboratory Life: The Construction of Scientific Facts*. Princeton UP, 1979.

Leaker, Cathy, and Heather Ostman. "Composing Knowledge: Writing, Rhetoric, and Reflection in Prior Learning Assessment." *College Composition and Communication*, vol. 61, no. 4, 2010, pp. 691–717.

Lynch, Sarah N., and Reade Levinson. "Attorney General Sessions Limits Asylum for Domestic Violence Victims." *Reuters*, 11 Jun. 2018, https://www.reuters.com/article/us-usa-sessions-asylum-idUSKBN1J72HP.

Rose, Mike. *Why School?: Reclaiming Education for All of Us*. The New Press, 2009.

Villegas, Malia, et al. *Knowledge and Education*. Harvard Educational Review, 2008.

Yancey, Kathleen Blake. "Postmodernism, Palimpsest and Portfolios: Theoretical Issues in the Representation of Student Work." *College Composition and Communication* vol. 55, no. 4 (2004): 738–761.

Yancey, Kathleen Blake. *Reflection in the Writing Classroom*. Utah State University Press, 1998.

INDEX

ABOUT THE AUTHORS

Tuli Chatterji is associate professor in the Department of English at LaGuardia Community College of City University of New York. Her research interests include postcolonial literature, South Asian queer studies, and composition theory and pedagogy. She lives in Long Island, New York, with her family.

Katie Daily is lecturer of English and Allston Burr resident dean at Harvard University. Previously, Katie spent four years as an assistant professor of English and associate dean at West Point. Her book, *Rejection and Disaffiliation in Twenty-First Century American Immigration Narratives,* was published by Palgrave in 2018.

Libby Garland teaches history at Kingsborough Community College of the City University of New York, as well as at the City University of New York Graduate Center. She is the author of *After They Closed the Gates: Jewish Illegal Immigration to the United States, 1921–1965* (University of Chicago Press, 2014).

Silvia Giagnoni is the author of *Here We May Rest. Alabama Immigrants in the Age of HB 56* (NewSouth Press, 2017); *Oltre la Siepe. Alla Ricerca di Harper Lee* (Edizioni dell'Asino 2013); and *Fields of Resistance. The Struggle of Florida's Farmworkers for Justice* (Haymarket Books, 2011). Her first work of fiction is forthcoming for Iacobelli Editore (Spring 2021).

Sibylle Gruber is professor of rhetoric, writing, and digital media studies at Northern Arizona University. She has published on the positionalities of international faculty, feminist rhetorics, technological literacies, composition theories and practices, and cultural studies. Her current work addresses how communication practices influence self-perception and other-perception. She teaches courses that focus on the social and cultural aspects of communicative practices.

John C. Havard is professor of English at Kennesaw State University, specializing in early American literature and multiethnic and Latinx literatures. He is the author of *Hispanicism and Early US Literature* (University of Alabama Press, 2018).

Timothy J. Henderson is a historian and the author of several books on the history of Mexico, including *Beyond Borders: A History of Mexican Immigration to the United States* (2011).

Brennan Herring received his Bachelor of Science in Business Administration in marketing from the Auburn University at Montgomery College of Business in 2019. He was a member of the University Honors Program and currently works in marketing and customer experience roles in the Montgomery, Alabama area.

Danizete Martínez teaches a cross-cultural and regionally driven composition pedagogy at Central New Mexico Community College. She has recently published the chapter "Teaching Chicana Literature in Community College: Social, Ethnic, and Linguistic Hybridity in Ana Castillo's So Far from God" in the first edited collection on the author.

Lilian W. Mina is associate professor of English and the Director of Composition at Auburn University at Montgomery. She researches digital rhetoric with focus on multimodal composing and writing teachers' use of digital technologies as well as (technology) professional development of writing teachers. Her work has appeared in multiple journals and edited collections.

Heather Ostman is professor of English and director of the Humanities Institute at SUNY Westchester Community College, where she teaches writing and literature. In addition to authoring several articles on American literature and writing pedagogy, she is the author of *Kate Chopin and Catholicism* (Palgrave Macmillan, 2020), *The Fiction of Junot Díaz* (Rowman and Littlefield, 2017), and *Writing Program Administration and the Community College* (Parlor Press, 2013); she has also edited three essay collections on the fiction of Kate Chopin.

Rachel Pate graduated from Auburn University at Montgomery in May 2019 majoring in Spanish language with a minor in international studies, focused on Mexican history and culture. She now teaches Spanish in a public high school outside of Tuscaloosa, Alabama, where she resides with her husband as she continues her education.

Emily Schnee is professor of English at Kingsborough Community College, City University of New York. Her research focuses on questions of justice and equity in community college education and has been published in *Community College Journal of Research and Practice*, *Radical Teacher*, *Community College Review*, *Teachers College Record*, and other journals.

Elizabeth Stone, professor of English at Fordham University, teaches the literature of twentieth- and twenty-first-century immigration, and writes about immigration for scholarly journals and national publications, including *The New York Times*. Immigration stories are included in her book, *Black Sheep and Kissing Cousins: How Our Family Stories Shape Us* (Routledge, 2004).

Howard Tinberg, professor of English at Bristol Community College, Mass., is the author of *Border Talk: Writing and Knowing in the Two-Year College* and *Writing with Consequence: What Writing Does in the Disciplines*. He is co-author of *The Community College Writer: Exceeding Expectations*, and *Teaching, Learning and the Holocaust: An Integrative Approach*. He is co-editor of *Deep Reading: Teaching Reading in the Writing Classroom*, (CCCC Outstanding Book Award, Edited Collection), *What Is "College-Level" Writing?*, and *What is "College-Level" Writing?*, Vol 2.